CAMPUS GHOSTS OF NORMAN, OKLAHOMA

CAMPUS GHOSTS OF NORMAN, OKLAHOMA

JEFF PROVINE

Haunted America

Published by Haunted America
A Division of The History Press
Charleston, SC 29403
www.historypress.net

All photos taken by author unless otherwise noted.

First published 2013

Manufactured in the United States

ISBN 978.1.62619.212.6

Library of Congress CIP data applied for.

Notice: The information in this book is true and complete to the best of our knowledge. It is offered without guarantee on the part of the author or The History Press. The author and The History Press disclaim all liability in connection with the use of this book.

To Tess, for suggesting I hunt ghosts.

CONTENTS

PREFACE

While backpacking in Britain in 2009, I took every ghost tour I could find. There were plenty of them; a country one thousand years old has had a plethora of dead people. Taking into account Jack the Ripper's mass murders in London and the vaults of Edinburgh, where hundreds met their doom during the Great Fire of 1824, there seemed to be no end to the ghosts and eerie tales.

I followed my friend Tess on a hometown ghost tour on the Isle of Wight. In this town where she had spent much of her life, there were piles of ghosts. A weeping young mother still walks the stream where her child drowned, a government office is haunted by a worker stressed to suicide and a butcher shop rests at the crossroads corner where hangings took place for centuries. During my time staying on the island, we had driven by that stream and those buildings and that shop a number of times. Ghosts were everywhere!

Feeling a little "ghost envy," I told Tess the one ghost story I knew about Norman, Oklahoma, where I had spent the last few years in college. There was the spirit of a little boy roller skating in Ellison Hall, which used to be a hospital.

She replied, "That's great! You should do a Norman ghost tour!"

I scoffed. Everything in Oklahoma, other than a few buffalo wallows, is at most 130 years old. There hasn't been much time for people to be here, let alone ghosts.

When I returned to teach classes that fall, Tess's enthusiastic suggestion haunted me. In my free time during office hours, I began researching rumors and asking around campus if anyone had a ghost story. On top of the one I knew, I had more than a dozen within a few weeks. Buildings I had walked past every day of my career in higher education had harrowing tales that I had never even imagined: exorcism, beheading, disembodied whispers, named spirits and roaming ones.

That Halloween, I led a tour for friends and family. The next Halloween, I led tours for friends of friends stretching to dozens. The next Halloween, hundreds showed up to hear ghost stories. The OU Visitor Center asked me to make tours monthly, weather permitting, and it has become a facet of the university, with more than two thousand attendees.

All of it came from simply asking about the hidden stories of our world. Every corner has its shadow, and we never know what we may learn if we peer into them.

ACKNOWLEDGEMENTS

I'd like to give a special thanks to all those who helped in the research for this book by offering their time for interviews. Paranormal investigation teams—including the Contact Research Investigation Specialists, Society of the Haunted and Paranormal Times Research Society—were instrumental in describing elements of parapsychology and giving scientific perspectives to historical anecdotes. Library staff at the Bizzell Memorial Library, Western Histories Collection, and the Norman Historical Society gave excellent instruction on researching newspaper archives and campus materials. Those at Bizzell also provided fascinating information about their own famous ghost. Thanks to the members of Chi Omega, Delta Gamma and Triangle, who were happy to share their experiences and stories of brothers and sisters past. Thanks to all of these facilities' management staffs, secretaries, public relations liaisons and employees who took time out of their busy schedules for interviews. In addition to the university, I would like to thank Keith F. Walker Oil & Gas Company, the Boyd Street Marines recruitment office, Café Plaid and the Norman Police Department for their helpful assistance. And a special thanks goes to all of the students, both present and alumni, who help make Norman the college town it is.

Everyone has a story to tell. I'm blessed to have heard so many.

INTRODUCTION

The city of Norman, Oklahoma, was settled in 1889 by "land run," a method of colonization rarely seen before or since. Before April 22, the town had been nothing but empty plots and wooden stakes posted by the U.S. Army Corps of Engineers. By the night after, Norman had a population of 150 permanent residents. By April 23, downtown was already being construction, and the population had climbed to thousands. Norman was one of many towns settled throughout the "Unassigned Lands" that would become part of Oklahoma Territory, but newly local businessmen had a plan to make the town great.

With such spontaneous growth, the territory was packed with contests for the seat of government, which would not only be prosperous as a center of revenue but also hold a great deal of sway over other communities. Norman decided to campaign for the territorial university instead, winning a special niche while other towns, such as Guthrie and Oklahoma City, battled for supremacy. Norman Territorial University eventually changed its official name to the University of Oklahoma (OU), but the campus always remained a part of the community. Even in 1903, when much of the campus burned down and nearly wiped out a decade of work, Norman brushed away bids by other towns to host the university with new facilities. Norman had made the pledge to be a college town, and it aimed to keep it.

Over its century-long history, the collegiate community around Norman has expanded greatly. From a single building on a treeless plain, Norman now has a campus cascading nearly two miles from the original home of

OU's first president, David Ross Boyd, to the research campus housing the National Weather Center. Along its west side, rows of Greek fraternities and sororities rest. To the north, several blocks of shops and restaurants known as Campus Corner have served students as long as they have been in Norman.

Amid football games and classes, college life rolls on, often not even letting death stop it. Campus is famous for its library ghost, and many people might even have heard of the roller skating little boy ghost, but there are darker tales, too. A malicious ghost was exorcized in 1973 after attacking a student. In a terrible accident, the angry spirit of a young man haunts a cafeteria basement. A professor of the organ still critiques students. A restaurant's bakery has a supernatural presence. And a halfway home for the mentally ill is still believed to have residents despite being closed down after grisly deaths.

Yet not all ghosts are negative. Many are simply talkative or a little rambunctious, at most pulling pranks, causing suspicious sounds or turning the lights back on. Some spirits are even positive, as with a sorority girl dead for more than forty years who still looks after her fellow sisters.

Whether benevolent, nasty or just a little strange, the school spirit in Norman never dies.

Part I
Hallowed Halls

Every school has its legends, and Norman's University of Oklahoma is no exception. There are tales of rats the size of dogs in the utility tunnels that connect all of the buildings with pipes and cables. Other whispers point to forbidden experiments or believe that the ghost of Jimi Hendrix appears on the back of a statue.

Yet, strangely, many of these stories are rooted in truth. Jimi Hendrix did perform in Norman for one of his last concerts before flying in 1970 to London, where he was discovered dead from barbiturate overdose. There is the shadow of a face on the back of the William Bizzell statue whispered to be the face of his spirit, but actually the stain is from stenciled spray paint rather than ectoplasm. A student graffitied "Free Leonard" there with a silhouette of Leonard Peltier, a Native American believed to be wrongly imprisoned for murder after the shootout on the Pine Ridge Indian Reservation in 1975.

Another famous campus legend is the curse of the library clock tower, noting that students who walk underneath it will not graduate in four years. According to a running informal poll of graduates who visit campus, the curse holds a 92 percent accuracy rate. One can argue about the socioeconomic changes of the college environment requiring more time due to students working while in school or participating in internships and study abroad on a wider scale, or the psychology of people who walk under clock towers, but the "curse" explanation is by far the most popular.

Other legends are also partially true, such as the statute of a rearing horse near the Fred Jones Jr. Museum of Art. Affectionately known to students as

The library clock tower, cursed so that students who walk under it won't graduate in four years.

the "demon horse," the blue and white fiberglass statue with huge glowing red eyes is intimidating. Students whisper to one another that it killed its own creator. Its actual title is *Mesteño* ("Mustang") by artist Luis Jimenez, and it served as the model for the three-story *Blue Mustang* that stands outside the Denver airport. On June 13, 2006, during *Blue Mustang*'s construction, a piece broke loose in Jimenez's studio, pinning him and severing an artery. Jimenez did not survive the accident, but his statue was later completed by his family and installed. Some Denverites believe it to be cursed, just as Normanites are wary of their own *Mesteño*.

The Spoon Holder—a round, gray concrete bench handcrafted as a gift from the class of 1910—sits as a landmark in the middle of the North Oval. It was constructed from handfuls of concrete by seniors over the course of a single night to surprise the school the next morning. According to campus legend, couples who kiss (or "spoon," as the term in 1910 meant) in the Spoon Holder are destined to be married. While one of the more heartwarming campus legends, it has been debunked on a number of occasions. Perhaps the myth is perpetuated as an excuse for free kisses.

With the spectrum of gray that exists between fact and fiction, it is difficult to sort out the truth about the many stories surrounding the university. Skepticism is key to a good ghost story, demonstrating what

The Spoonholder, where students who kiss are believed to eventually get married.

may be proven and causing one to shrug unknowingly at those things that are unexplainable. There are, in fact, things that go bump in the night without justification beyond the paranormal, and the campus in Norman has a healthy share.

Fires

Evans Hall

The first major building constructed on campus in Norman was called University Hall, completed in 1893 just after the University of Oklahoma came into being. Before then, classes had taken place around Norman, including what was known as the Rock Building on Main Street. Aside from the one multistory brick building, the campus consisted of a few temporary wood-frame buildings and a larger gymnasium. University Hall became the prize of the south end of Norman, showing what could be done with hard work and optimism. As the college grew, so did the aspirations for the future, and a second building began going up in 1902. As the new "University Hall" neared completion in early 1903, the school renamed its old building "Science Hall" and transferred all of its important collections there: laboratory equipment, administrative documents and more than ten thousand specimens that had been collected in the school's herbarium by the young professor of chemistry and biology Edwin DeBarr and head of botany Dr. Albert Heald Van Vleet, the first faculty member at OU to hold a doctorate. The days ahead seemed bright for the young university.

Then, on January 6, 1903, tragedy struck the campus. A night watchman noticed light flickering in what was now known as Science Hall, a little northwest of where the new University Hall was still under construction. The Norman Fire Department was summoned, even though campus was at that time outside city limits. Fire hydrants did not exist anywhere near the hall, and frantic bystanders began organizing a bucket brigade. Suddenly, the slowly burning building began to explode into flames in front of them. The wooden floors had recently been oiled, causing the fire to spread faster than anyone could think of stopping it.

The matter then became saving as much of the school's materials as possible. Students found a ladder and climbed into the window of President

Boyd's office. There, they grabbed every paper they could find and threw them out to people below, who collected them, saving items such as grade records, financial sheets and even personal letters. Other students ventured down into the basement, snatching up valuable chemicals and instruments from the laboratory there and carrying them to safety. Still others broke into every lecture room not on fire and saved maps, books, animal hides, anything that could be easily carried. President Boyd himself charged into the burning building, but he collapsed due to smoke inhalation and suffered "sore lungs" for weeks.

After only a few hours, the entire building was destroyed. The university's library of more than twelve thousand volumes was gone, except for what had been checked out to students. Along with the books went the herbarium, the geological collection and prepared lectures—an entire decade's worth of collegiate research and growth. Losses were calculated at $84,000; insurance would only pay $35,000 for the building. Boyd and the regents immediately put the money toward beginning a new Science Hall, which stands at the southwest corner of the North Oval today.

Hope for the time was put into the new University Hall, which contractors eagerly swore to complete within the month before classes started February 2. It was actually completed on March 16, but students and faculty made do with what they had. While the building was designed in the Federal style, with huge columns and an enormous dome, money concerns caused them to cancel plans of building a west wing, giving the building a lopsided, almost amputated, look. The city of Norman stepped up to aid the devastated university. Every church and club hall in town volunteered space for classes, storage and office use.

Meanwhile, other communities in the state began offering a different form of aid by suggesting that Norman give up the university to them. Town leaders came to Norman and offered to take the burden of a nearly ruined university off their hands. Kingfisher, northwest of Oklahoma City, even wrote up a check for $10,000 to reimburse the City of Norman for investments in the university. Norman refused, and it remains a college town to this day.

The new University Hall was soon joined in 1904 by a new Science Building and a Carnegie Library building, paid for by the charity of the Scottish steel magnate. The university expanded rapidly with a new music department, fraternal organizations and growth of its football program under a young Benjamin "Bennie" Owens. By 1907, as the university shut down for winter break, the future seemed bright once more.

Then, on December 20, fiery tragedy struck again. Only a few students were still in town, the rest having already caught the train for home. Buildings had been closed, and University Hall was undergoing renovations, with a new coat of paint on the white dome. As it was a cold day, the painters set up a gasoline stove inside the wooden dome to warm the linseed oil to be used as sealant for the paint. In the middle of the afternoon, something caused the stove to burst. Flames surged up the dome, giving off a huge plume of smoke.

Students who had been waiting to leave rushed back to campus alongside curious Normanites. While they attempted to find hoses long enough and in good enough repair to put out the fire, the dome burned and then buckled. It fell through the roof, through two floors of the building and down to the basement. Oil-fed flames surged through the wood-floored hallways. For the second time, University Hall was pushed past the brink of destruction.

Also for the second time, students literally leaped into the flames to save their school. Pianos were dragged out of the new Fine Arts department rooms and rolled onto the grassy lawn. Furniture in rooms outfitted by donations from the local YMCA were tossed out the windows and saved. Whatever students could find, they dragged out of the building before the flames became so hot that walls began to collapse. Two students were injured: one by a chair thrown from a window and another by broken glass—both caused by the earnestness of saving what could be saved out of the doomed building.

Even as the flames were still dying, President Boyd began plans to reopen the school on January 6. Classes would be held in the Science Hall and library. Money from the insurance would be invested in a new University Hall, later known as Evans Hall after the university's second president. This third administration building was built out of fireproof brick and stands resilient to this day.

Although the building is in no danger of burning as its predecessors did, rumors on campus talk of a ghost still panicked about getting out. The entrance to the north in the alley behind the Bizzell Memorial Library consists of two pairs of heavy wooden, glass and brass doors. One is set inside the other, creating a small foyer that keeps out gusts of cold air. According to students who say they've heard it, the inner doors sometimes rattle intensely and even open themselves. It is as if something is trying to break out. "It's just the wind" is the clichéd response to explain the ghostly noise, even though the doors are protected from gusts by the buildings around them.

Evans Hall, the third building to be known as University Hall.

The rumors go on to say that in the burning of the old University Halls, several students perished, and these are their spirits still attempting to escape the flaming wreckage. Stories paint pictures of panicked students finding the doors locked and throwing themselves against the wooden barriers before succumbing to flame and smoke. Even with the building gone, they still find themselves trapped in a cycle of existence, never able to escape torment as the burning building consumed them.

In both historical fires, no one was injured beyond cuts, bruises and President Boyd's sore lungs. Instead of a conscious or semiconscious spirit reliving the final nightmare of its life, parapsychologists offer the suggestion of a psychological imprint. The fervent energy is not a panicked escape but rather the memory of collegiate heroism played out. Rather than student spirits attempting to break out, the doors may rattle as the shades of alumni long past attempt to break *in* to protect their school from any danger.

A GHOSTLY ORGANIST

Reynolds Performing Arts Center

While most of the buildings on the University of Oklahoma's North Oval sit flush with the street, something resembling a cathedral sits back from the sidewalk, as if gracefully reclined. During his visit, famed architect Frank Lloyd Wright dubbed the building "Cherokee Gothic," a style applied to all buildings newly built on campus. It features dark and pale bricks with a decorative Gothic façade, completed by light-gray stone buttresses and statues. Four huge, heavy wooden doors lead into the spacious lobby, with symmetrical stairs leading to the balcony. A wide mural shows some of the famous faces of OU, from presidents to musicians to actors. Among them is a haunting, half-turned figure of an organist expertly plying her craft. Just as in her portrait, Professor Mildred Andrews Boggess still contributes to the university despite her death.

The Fine Arts program began with a call from the first president, David Ross Boyd, to a Swedish immigrant violin teacher living in Kansas, Fredrik Holmberg. He had come to the United States as a teenager and worked his way through Bethany College by manual farm labor. He upheld a dedication to music almost to the level of religion, believing it to be one of the most powerful forces to bring community to what would otherwise be an impassionate group of humans.

Holmberg answered Boyd's call and arrived in Norman by train in 1903. In the midst of a dust storm, he spotted a cluster of buildings that looked like a college campus. After hiking more than a mile to the territorial mental hospital, Holmberg realized his mistake. He crossed town on foot again, finally coming upon the fledgling University of Oklahoma's one building, with only one wing completed. Nearly five miles on foot in a barren, dusty landscape to a university without even a whole building prompted Holmberg to prepare his resignation.

Instead, he was greeted by Boyd, so ecstatic to see him that Holmberg didn't have the opportunity to resign before the president had inspired him with his plans for the university. Holmberg later wrote that Boyd "had a way of giving one an optimistic outlook" as he eagerly pointed out spots for new buildings and ideas for the School of Fine Arts. Holmberg was persuaded to stay and applied his own dedication to the campus, organizing glee clubs for men and women, a band, an orchestra and an oratorio chorus, all within his first six weeks. By 1909, he was made

Holmberg Hall, once "the Auditorium" on campus.

dean of Fine Arts, which would in 1924 become its own college within the university.

The performers needed a place of their own, and as World War I came to a close, construction was completed on a hall fitted with a theater with seating for hundreds. Originally dubbed "the Auditorium," students wanted to show their appreciation to Holmberg and began a petition to name the building in his honor. Holmberg balked and refused the idea that a building should be named for a living person. He passed away in 1936, never retiring and still at work as dean, and in 1938, the state regents voted to rename the Auditorium "Holmberg Hall."

That same year, Fine Arts hired a twenty-three-year-old organist who would make her own mark on the school. Professor Mildred Andrews Boggess had studied as an undergraduate in Oklahoma but went on to Michigan for her postgraduate work studying music, specifically the organ. She was a talented organist who could have gained great fame and fortune as a professional performer, but Boggess dedicated her life to building up graduate-level organ studies at the university. Despite her slim stature, she

Left: The Auditorium/Holmberg Hall.

Right: The Memorial Organ, named in honor of Mildred Andrews Boggess.

held a potent Type A personality that some might whisper as "tyrannical," although never in her presence.

Boggess was relentless in her determination. During her thirty-eight-year tenure, she established an unbeatable record for mentoring the highest number of national-level organ players and champions. Even after her entry into the Oklahoma Hall of Fame and retirement, she continued to perform for the university. In her will, she set aside a good deal of her estate to begin the fund for the cathedral organ she felt the university lacked. Fundraising fulfilled her dream, and the organ now stands in Catlett Hall in her honor. Boggess passed away in 1987, but in many ways, she never left the campus.

In 2002, renovations began on Holmberg Hall. A grant had been gifted for the joining of the old auditorium with newer theaters to form the sprawling Reynolds Performing Arts Center. Parapsychologists note that renovations and construction activity "stir up" paranormal activity, and it seemed that Holmberg was no exception. During the reconstruction, one of the old organs was moved out of its place, and strange things began to happen.

Tools went missing despite security around the worksite. Demolition was delayed by unexplained electrical problems. Odd noises rang through the halls. Workers began quitting the site, dubbing it "haunted" or even "cursed." Despite the disruptions, work was finally finished in 2005. To this day, strange activity continues, and overlapping stories have caused the student body to suggest that Professor Boggess is still around.

During practices and even performances, students are often interrupted by the jarring sound of a slammed door. Most of the cases are written off as someone failing to catch the door as they sneaked out to take a call or stretch their legs. However, the slamming sound happens even as students practice on their own time, alone in the auditorium. The interruption causes them to break focus and have to start over, much as if someone were attempting to show them where they have gone wrong and pressing them to work harder for perfection.

People sensitive to impressions given by rooms or buildings note that there is a strange "vibe" about Holmberg Hall. It gives the sense of being watched, perhaps judged, even though the person is positive in being the only mortal in the room or hall. A particularly strong sensation comes from the

The stage lights where Boggess is said to appear.

auditorium, with its windowless walls and curtains that look as if something could be hiding just beyond them.

Most famously, according to campus legend, students on stage can look up into the stage lights to see a matronly visage looking down on them. The woman is described as older, with something of a stern face ringed by full, gray hair. Even students who have never heard of Professor Boggess claim to have seen the image as described and agree that it could have been someone like her when shown a photograph.

Other rumors about Holmberg Hall offer that organ music can be heard playing through the building. Upon hearing the sound, casual visitors simply tell themselves, "Oh, it's one of the practice rooms."

While the Reynolds Center does have more than fifty practice rooms, they are all heavily insulated to prevent noise. In addition, each room is fitted with a piano, either upright or grand—*not* an organ. The sounds have also been attributed to pranks or just Holmberg being an old building, but others feel that Boggess continues to practice in the auditorium as she had for more than fifty years. Perhaps Professor Boggess still roams the practice rooms and the theater of what has become the Reynolds Performing Arts Center. Even from beyond the grave, she still pushes her students to do their very best, no matter the cost of discipline.

Mildred Andrews Boggess, a feature on the mural inside Holmberg.

Beyond the old Holmberg Hall, on the west end of the Reynolds Performing Arts Center, the Rupel Jones Theatre has a spirit of its own. According to students in the drama department of the College of Fine Arts, something has taken up residence in the theater and causes inexplicable noises. Most commonly heard are the sounds of footsteps walking across the stage. In front of many witnesses, heavy footfalls clunk back and forth, even though every eye can see that the stage is empty.

The nearby restrooms also carry paranormal activity, causing the doors to the stalls to slam. The sound has startled people outside the restrooms when they are empty, and those visiting them have even witnessed the sudden movement of the doors. One might wonder whether the doors are simply set at an aggressive angle on their hinges, but the doors slam themselves closed as well as open. Poorly weighted hinges could not work both ways.

The lighting booth is also believed to be haunted. Crew members who sit there during practices and performances say that they can feel a presence, as if someone were standing behind or beside them, watching the play along with them. Despite being elevated where it should catch the rising warm air, the booth is at times very cold. No one is sure what ghost might have come into the theater, but it seems as interested in the arts as Professor Boggess herself.

SCIENTISTS AND A FIREBUG

Chemistry Building

A stern gray building labeled "Chemistry" stands as it has since 1916 on the North Oval, peering out quietly from behind trees and well-groomed shrubs. It is one of the early buildings on campus, dating from before the time of the established Cherokee Gothic architecture with red brick and light-gray trim that has become synonymous with the campus. Its plain face is decorated with intricate carvings and false pillars, creating an air of subtle majesty and mystery about the Chemistry Building. Built to house the rapidly growing chemistry department after $100,000 had been raised in 1913, it was named for its potent supporter, Edwin C. DeBarr.

DeBarr was a brilliant teacher and scientist who came to the university as one of the four original faculty. He had collected an impressive array of degrees, including a bachelor's in education, a master's in chemistry and another bachelor's (in pharmacy) before achieving his PhD. As the student body began to grow on campus, he taught a wide range of classes, including biology, chemistry and medicine.

While he contributed a great deal to the founding of the school, DeBarr seemed reluctant to relinquish any power he assembled. He established the School of Pharmacy, for which he was dean; headed the School of Chemical Engineering; and also served as the first vice-president for fifteen years, although he had campaigned to also lead the graduate school. The Chemistry Building was his brainchild, and he is believed to have sketched what he wanted before giving designs over to the architectural firm. In addition to all his academic work, the popular "Daddy DeBarr" led the hymns during chapel services and influenced local politics.

In 1923, Oklahoma began a campaign against the ultraconservative racist secret society known as the Ku Klux Klan. While wearing masks, these men went about conducting acts of terrorism to keep those they considered "lesser" from reaching places of prominence. Even when not wearing their masks, the Klansmen acted with social and political pressure to put forth their own agenda.

As part of its counterstrike following the impeachment of Governor John C. Walton for his martial law crackdown after interracial violence tore apart the people, the Oklahoma state legislature passed the Anti-Mask Law. The new law, still on the books today, made it illegal in the state to wear a mask on any day other than Halloween. Punishments included fines, jail time and, perhaps most notable for someone attempting to hide

The old Chemistry Building.

his identity, publication of the criminal's name in the "Legals" section of the local newspaper. Other fraternal organizations also fell under the Anti-Mask Law, creating a new wave of transparency.

Also in 1923, DeBarr's connections with the Ku Klux Klan became apparent. In July, he was dismissed after a number of cases came forth. He espoused his distrust of Catholicism and made arguments for the inferiority of other races, but it was his politicking behind the backs of other administrators when OU president Brooks had been away on campus that led to his end. Later, it was shown that his connections to the Klan were very deep: he had been elected grand dragon of Oklahoma the year before. After his dismissal, he would become the national chaplain for the Klan, with the title "Imperial Kludd."

In response to his dismissal, DeBarr said simply, "I have been greatly misrepresented. If thirty years of living and doing in Norman and Oklahoma are not a sufficient defense, then I have no other to make." He wished to stand on his accomplishments, but there was no way to separate the devious foundation on which those accomplishments were built.

Although the university had separated itself from DeBarr, his name remained on the building he helped to erect. In 1988, a sit-in by students prompted action by the state regents to officially strip his name from the building. Ever since the protest, it has been simply known as "Chemistry." A block-long stretch of road in Campus Corner still bears his name, DeBarr Avenue.

Even beyond its troubled history from the name that once stood on the building, Chemistry has a number of strange residents, one potentially malicious. Since the days of DeBarr, the chemistry department has blossomed and now resides to the south of the main campus in a new building. The Chemistry Building still holds room for labs and offices, filling up the annex that connects it with the massive Physical Science Center to the west. The Blender (PSC) had been built in the 1970s as part of the push for more space for hard sciences. The push continues, and Chemistry has been largely left behind. In the case of the fourth floor, it has been shut off completely.

To reach the fourth floor of the Chemistry Building, a visitor must pick one of three stairwells, as the others connect only with the annex, creating a sort of vertical maze. Labs are still used on the second and third floors, but the fourth was found to contain asbestos in the walls. Asbestos, which was praised for its heat-retardant attributes before its discovery as a carcinogen was made, proved to be far more dangerous than beneficial to mankind and can no longer be used in construction. Removing it is costly

Stairway to the fourth floor, which contains a jog in the ceiling due to the roof.

due to its hazardous nature, and many institutions find that it is best to close off the asbestos-laden rooms until funds are more widely available.

Visitors can still climb the several flights up to the fourth floor, where the top half-floor of Chemistry causes the ceiling to have a blocky bulge that has to be ducked under. The air is thick due to the sealed-off ventilation that is keeping the asbestos safely locked away and the heat from below from wafting upward. From the small lobby, currently marked by caution tape, a door leading south warns visitors that it is not to be opened except by authorized staff with proper equipment. The door has a narrow window leading to the dark, abandoned laboratory inside.

Since it was closed off quickly to ensure safety, the lab is left in the same condition it has been for decades. Original wooden chemical hoods stand in the center of undisturbed long tables. Antique glassware sleeps along with preserved equipment. Even old newspapers are spread out where they were being read years ago. Dust has settled in the room, where it rests without any breeze to disturb it.

Yet things are known to move around the old laboratory. Despite the door being locked and almost no exposure to outside air, people passing by peek inside to notice that the newspaper pages have been flipped, as if someone were rereading it again and again. Neat stacks of dust have been swept away from where they once lay.

Skeptics argue that pests such as mice, unaware of the dangers of asbestos, may scurry inside and move the papers or dust. While the argument is very reasonable, others have reported that the laboratory equipment itself has been moved. No one confesses to having witnessed movement, but there have been several cases in which viewers agree that the apparatuses in the lab take up different positions.

Above: The south laboratory, closed up for half a century.

Left: Halls notorious for fires.

In addition to the haunted fourth-floor laboratory, the annex has its own, less careful peculiar activity. While there have been numerous cases of fire on campus since the destruction of the first University Hall in 1903 (and the second in 1907), nowhere has had more uncontrolled burns than the Chemistry annex. It is reasonable to assume that other buildings do not have as much danger as laboratories with Bunsen burners and natural gas connections, but the unpredictability of the fires has convinced many in the annex that they have a pyromaniac ghost.

Despite careful laboratory practices and training, the fire department routinely appears at the annex to put out a blaze or check up on someone who had to make use of the fire extinguishers and hoses. Lab workers swear that they made certain they had turned off their equipment and then saw it light up in a new fire. In other cases, people were using such small flames without anything flammable around that the fire could not have possibly spread. Nonetheless, whether through malicious activity or simply pranks, the jets have been witnessed turning themselves up. A lab worker may turn his back for a moment and then return to see papers that had been across the table suddenly tucked up next to the burner.

In addition to fire, the annex has been notorious for other activity often related to poltergeists. The electrical system flickers, and bulbs burn out far faster than they should. As with many buildings on campus, the hallways are fitted with automatic doors and motion-sensor lights. Even though no person is around, doors are known to open by themselves. People in their offices will see hallway lights turn on, but when they come out to see who is wandering campus so late at night, no one will be walking there.

It is unknown whether any of the ghostly activity around Chemistry is related to Edwin DeBarr, its infamous champion. One could imagine his spirit, restless from his early dismissal, revisits the building that he once held so dearly. With his chemical knowledge, he would certainly be at home in the fourth-floor laboratory, quietly spending eternity with his apparatuses and a few old papers.

Morgues and Roller Skates

Ellison Hall

The campus's first infirmary was completed in 1928 and dubbed Hygeia Hall after the Greek goddess of health. It was renamed Ellison Hall soon thereafter in 1932 in honor of Director of Student Health Dr. Gayfree Ellison. He was popular with the students, although he quickly caught the blame when any illness was not immediately resolved.

One of Ellison's first crises as director was an epidemic of smallpox that ran through the state in 1922. Nearby Potawatomie County was quarantined, but the disease came to Norman as well, supposedly carried by a traveling salesman specializing in jewelry. In the end, five people died in the town.

Ellison, a microbiologist in addition to his work directing student health, encouraged vaccination and stated that any misgivings about the vaccine were based in ignorance. Soon the entire city began a vaccination drive, with citizens volunteering themselves and community groups donating vaccines. The university required students to take the weakened virus that would prevent them from suffering the full strike of the terrible disease. Some doctors, including Ellison, even recommended being vaccinated twice to ensure the body's immune system became adapted to smallpox.

Ellison Hall, once the campus's infirmary.

In November, as the disease spread, rumors ran wild. Some said that the smallpox epidemic was, in fact, the black plague, the same that had wiped out one-third of Europe. Other rumors stated that it was far worse than city health officials made known and that some thirty-nine people had been secretly quarantined. In fact, only a dozen cases were confirmed. More rumors believed that Norman would be quarantined, such as a farmer mentioning his "last trip" into Norman before the city was to be walled off. A rumor flashed through the Greeks on campus that Norman would be closed at midnight on Monday, November 29, just before students would be heading home for Thanksgiving break. According to the *Norman Transcript*'s coverage of the panic, "Several members of one sorority… took the midnight train to Ardmore, called Norman the next morning, discovered their mistake, and sheepishly returned Tuesday afternoon." Another sorority girl angrily called Dr. Ellison at 3:00 a.m., letting the phone ring until the weary university health officer answered. She demanded to know why he had warned other fraternities and sororities about such a citywide quarantine but not their house. He was dumbfounded by every ridiculous part of her outrage.

Five people in Norman died over the course of the epidemic, but students were young and healthy and readily improved. Five students were quarantined in late November, but by the middle of December, two had already been released and the others were already on the mend. The last student to catch smallpox was James LaMarr, an engineering senior, who believed that he was exposed to it during the Homecoming Parade. He had been vaccinated years before, so he put off getting a booster until he felt ill—by then, it was too late to stop it. Even so, according to Dr. Ellison, the case was less severe, as his body readily accepted the new vaccine.

In the 1950s, Ellison Hall served as the center for quarantine during a citywide epidemic. Polio struck all over the world, and Norman was no exception. In an interview with a woman who was fourteen at the time, she said that she spent a summer on the third floor with a set of boys, which she said was the worst part of having the disease, even more than the inflammation of her nervous system. Her biggest memory of the summer was sitting in the third-floor operating theater, facing a mirror that was arranged to look out the window. For hours while doctors drove needles into her back for spinal taps to alleviate the pressure of infected fluid, she stared back at the Gothic face of the library.

The most famous story of Ellison Hall's eerie past is of the roller skating boy. While the building was still known as Hygeia Hall, a little boy was roller skating on Elm Avenue, which lines the western side of campus and faces the

The wide windows of Ellison's surgical suites on the third floor.

infirmary. Versions of the story differ on whether he was hit by a car or had an asthma attack, but in both cases, he was in critical condition and rushed into Hygeia. They took him to the third floor, where the surgery suites were, and operated. The boy did not survive, but according to campus legend, he still plays in Ellison to this day.

In 1971, the Goddard Health Center opened across the street, updating and expanding health services for students. Ellison was occupied by the student government, which held its offices there until 2000. While the students worked, particularly at night, they would hear strange noises rolling up and down the third-floor hall. It would noticeably start on one side of the building, work its way down to the end and then come back. Others heard whispers and even giggles. Students passed on the story of the little boy from class to class, ensuring that everyone knew who the noisy culprit was.

When student government left for its new offices by the Union, the university's largest college, Arts & Sciences, took over the building. The antics of the little boy ghost continued. In an interview, one woman recalled the evening that she and a co-worker were staying late finishing a project on the third floor. They were alone, and the building was empty and quiet. Suddenly, down the hall, they heard a crash…and a giggle.

They turned to each other and agreed, "It's the ghost!" Her co-worker jumped up and locked the door.

"Why are you locking the door?" she called to her. "It's a ghost! Let's get out of here!" They left early that night and, since then, do their best not to work late.

Ellison has more than just the little boy and his roller skates, it seems. On the first floor, a woman in advising was working late one night when she heard voices down the hall. Thinking that some students had gotten in where they should not have, she left her office to chase them out. As soon as she came into the large meeting room where she had heard the voices, they stopped. She flipped on the light and called for them to come out, but no one was in the room. Becoming a little unnerved, she searched under the tables and behind chairs. She did not find anyone or any thing that could have made the commotion. She finally told herself that she had just imagined the sounds and went back to her office. After a few minutes, the voices came back. They were louder this time, "as if they were having a party." She left the office earlier than planned and has since transferred to a different department.

Several groups of paranormal investigators have explored Ellison Hall, including the Society of the Haunted on April 16, 2011. Two members of the society, Cathy Nance and Vanessa Hogle, are sensitive to psychic impressions. Their ability was described as the same emotional response that anyone might feel walking into a room. For examples, a happy, boisterous party gives a light and energetic mood, while dark, somber feelings settle on those in funeral parlors even without a funeral in session. They feel these impressions not only in the present but by "peeling back the layers of time."

A stairway known to creak even as no one living walks on it.

Without any knowledge of the building before, the team was led on a walk-through of the infirmary. On the third floor, both psychics felt a "strange energy" filled with sadness and great pain, yet there were also glimmers of hope. Cathy described her co-investigator Vanessa in her blog as looking "like she was almost in tears." She herself had images of torturous, crude equipment. Later, when told that the building was an infirmary, it became clear that these were impressions of the four surgery suites that outfitted the floor. Medical technology from the 1920s was certainly crude and perhaps barbaric by today's standards, but there was still the hope of recovery.

They also explored the basement, which had once served as the morgue. According to stories from Ellison's time as home for the student government, the large metal doors that led to the drawers where bodies were stored were still in the wall of the basement. They were kept locked, but every once in a while, someone would go down to the basement and find every single one of the metal doors standing open. The doors have since been removed and the spaces filled.

The basement holds a small hatch that leads to the utility tunnels that crisscross campus, running to every building. Both psychics noted dark feelings beyond that door. While Cathy was curious about it, Vanessa said that she would not go through that hatch for any reason. Something evil apparently lurked beyond. During their break and briefing session, it was explained that the building was an infirmary and that the basement had once been a morgue. Vanessa said that she didn't want to hear anything about dead bodies. In reply, on an EVP (electronic voice phenomenon) that may be found on the society website, a voice that does not belong to any of the investigation team or staff that guided them states, "I'm sorry."

In addition to psychic impressions, the team experienced a great deal of activity. Ellison's automatic lights are notorious for clicking on even when no one is around. During the visit, the light in the second-floor bathroom

Left: Once the morgue, the basement of Ellison now serves as more mundane storage.

Below: One of many entrances to the utility tunnels that run underground throughout the campus. According to rumor, students who enter the tunnels are immediately expelled.

turned itself on. Investigators rushed to check for any signs of ghosts. The team set up meters, attempting to detect shifts in electromagnetic fields, but whatever had set off the light had apparently moved on.

Throughout the night, the team heard knocks, footsteps and shuffling. Bumps and the sound of papers being moved rang from the office across from the bathroom on the second floor. They began to attempt to communicate with whatever was making the knock, asking, "If there is anyone there, tap on something to let us know." In one office, every time it was asked for, a knock was given.

Another series of knocks replied to the team's yes/no questions, much like playing Twenty Questions. They determined that the spirit was female and that she was trying to find a nurse. She also confirmed that there were more ghosts than just her in the building.

They heard other strange noises, including footsteps coming up the stairs from the first floor to the second. Cathy related that she even felt a gust of cold air pass by her, giving a sensation of bitter sadness that made tears flow down her cheeks. The famous sound of rolling wheels was also heard on the third floor, although Vanessa said that it seemed more like a gurney than roller skates.

On November 3, 2012, another paranormal investigation team, including Wayne Harris-Wyrick, spent an evening in Ellison. The team members encountered a few strange events, again including lights turning themselves on. EVPs from the investigation found male and female voices apparently replying to their comments, such as noting the ping-pong ball used to detect subtle movement. The light plastic balls are used in ghost hunting to determine whether something has moved through the area and can even be a focus of communication between mortals and those from beyond the veil. The ghosts did not seem to think much of it.

The clearest form of communication came when one of the female members of the group raised her hands. She announced to any spirits present that they could touch her if they wished. Her bracelet fell from her wrist, and she quickly revoked the offer.

A third team of investigators, Paranormal Times Research Society, spent two sessions in Ellison. During its first visit, the team members had a great deal of interaction with at least one ghost that was very willing to make itself known. Team members set up cameras in the conference room on the third floor, one of four rooms that had once been used for the old surgical suites. While they watched the monitors from another room, other members sat calmly around the conference table with the lights out. The investigation team began asking questions, attempting to make contact with the spirit believed to be the famous roller skating boy. One team member requested, "If someone is here, please give us a sign." The lights suddenly turned on.

The video from the investigation shows their eyes going wide and their jaws dropping. Everyone looks around at everyone else, no one expecting such a clear message. The room lights, not tied to a motion detector, had been turned on manually by some unseen hand.

Throughout the investigation, the spirit made further interaction with a light box that one of the investigators had brought with him. Like a flashlight, the box is designed to light up when it is pressed. The piece of equipment is popular with parapsychologists as it is carefully constructed to ensure that no other method such as a short across the wiring might cause it to light up. On a number of occasions, particularly when asked, the box lit up as if a hand had eagerly tapped it.

Hallway where a floating apparition appeared.

Additional EVPs were taken. A series of them confirmed the earlier investigators' interaction, as a ghostly voice was heard trying to call for a nurse. In the basement, there was another voice unheard by human ears but caught on audio equipment. It told them again and again that it had lost its keys and asked where it might find them.

On their second visit, in addition to noisy activity, the investigators claimed to have actually seen a ghost. Cameras were set up in hallways and open rooms throughout the building. While several of the investigators and their liaison with Arts & Sciences were watching the screen, a light moved through the doorway of the northeast conference room. They described what they saw as a "white body" and with the more formal term in parapsychology, "full body apparition." It had distinct arms and legs and seemed to glow with a pale light in the shadows. The light passed out of the conference room and into the hallway before disappearing again.

Leader Tanya McCoy radioed the other investigators in the building, asking if any of them had come out of the conference room. The replies came that the investigators on foot thought that *she* had been the one down the hall following *them*. They cleared up their confusion, but their amazement had only begun. Someone, or something, had appeared there, lingering for a moment as if it wanted to be seen and then disappeared.

Ellison Hall takes great pride in its ghostly residents, which tie it closely to the days of the building as the campus infirmary. As the ghosts do not seem to pose any harm, they are happy to work alongside them, even if they do often unlock the doors of their offices to find scattered papers.

THE MOST FAMOUS GHOST ON CAMPUS

The Library Decks

The Bizzell Memorial Library stands at the head of the South Oval, its Collegiate Gothic façade towering majestically as the behemoth structure rests behind. It was built in 1928 as the school's collection outgrew the Carnegie Library that had been donated a quarter century before. The library was built to include an enormous Great Reading Room, six levels of Decks—with nooks for studying amid thousands of volumes on metal shelves—and frosted glass floor plates that allow natural sunlight from the skylights above to flow down and save on electrical expenses.

Entrance to the Decks, believed to hold spirits among the thousands of books.

As the collection and student body continued to expand, so did the library. In 1958, an extension was completed, tripling the library space. Another extension grew in the 1980s, adding a clock tower, a sunken garden and even more space to satiate the exploding need for computers.

All of this new construction and the series of renovations between have turned the library into a sprawling maze with multiple floors (sometimes six, other times five), dead-end hallways and often confusing directions. Getting to the Oklahoma Canyon Garden includes going through an office and carefully around desks of workers. Many students believe that access to the garden is a myth until they see people there and then whisper down, as if the answer were forbidden, "How do you get in there?"

In addition to the mysteries of the library, it is also the most famous building for being haunted. Backward-walking guides enjoy mentioning "the library ghost" on the general tours for incoming freshmen and curious tourists. The story goes, according to who is telling it, that in the 1940s (or '30s, '50s or '60s), a student (sometimes male, sometimes female) was walking through the Decks when one of the glass plates came loose. He or she fell through and broke his or her neck. Now he or she roams the Decks, doomed to study for all time.

It makes for a great campus legend. All the pieces of the story are there, with the creepiness of the library and the sensation already that it seems haunted. The Decks of the library, nearly a century old, have low ceilings and narrow passages between the shelves. A nervous sense of claustrophobia will settle over anyone making his or her way through the books. Several stairwells have locked cages over them, preventing anyone except library staff from exploring the upper levels. Visitors may even see shadows as library patrons walk above them, seeming like disembodied footsteps through the frosted glass. When walking on the glass plates themselves, they can look down and nervously tap their toes, wondering just how stable the floor is after one hundred years.

Unfortunately for the story (but fortunately for its supposed victim), there does not seem to be any case of the glass plates breaking loose. During an interview with a library staff member who has worked there as an undergraduate, graduate and finally full-timer, he recalled a project attempting to search out the name of the library ghost. He and his co-

The Gothic face of the Bizzell Memorial Library.

Example of a replaced glass plate in the Decks.

workers in Periodicals spent their spare time carefully reading through every issue of the campus paper, the *Oklahoma Daily*. Through their efforts, they were unable to find any reference to a student dying in the library. While some suppose that it signals a coverup conspiracy, most agree that the story of a fall is just a myth.

Even if the library has never seen a victim, this is not to say that there is no library ghost. While some ghosts are stationary or fixed to a certain place, such as the young roller skating patient in the Ellison infirmary, other ghosts are transitive or wandering. Rather than a place becoming haunted simply out of a death, a ghost may meander there. Then, just as inexplicably, the spirit may leave.

The "wandering ghost" serves as a good explanation for much of the strange activity that has been known to happen in the oldest part of the library. Patrons note the sensation of being watched, but when they look around to see if someone is peering at them through the bookshelves, no one is there. In other instances, people will see the shadowy outlines of shoes on the glass plates above them, go upstairs and find no one standing there.

Footsteps are commonly heard in the Decks. It is an old building and somewhat cavernous without inner walls to stem the flow of sound, so echoes trickle along the brick outer walls. Even taking this into account, however, there are still strange instances of students hearing footsteps and then not seeing anyone to make them. Routinely in the Decks, someone studying or simply walking will hear another set of footsteps. They pause to look around the corner to make sure no one bumps into them, and they find nothing there. Other students claim to have been followed by footsteps or attempted to follow the footsteps themselves, ultimately finding nothing but cold air wafting with the rich smell of old books.

Some students claim to have heard whispers and even spoken voices in the Decks. The description usually makes the sound up to be a woman's voice, speaking words that are just beyond the edge of understanding. On a number of occasions, a student has heard a whisper and gotten up to see who was there. They search the aisles of books one by one and, one by one, find them empty.

Witnesses have experienced more than simple echoes or tricks to the ear. One graduate of the university who studied in the 1990s recalled the time she was seeking out a book in one of the lesser-visited corners of the Decks. She carefully perused the aisles, checking call numbers and titles in the search for her book. As she neared where it would be, there was a strange thump, and an entire shelf of books suddenly fell in front of her as if someone had struck it. Skeptics would wonder whether the shelving had been unstable, but the shelf itself did not give way. The student was convinced of paranormal activity and decided that she did not need that book after all.

Glass plates in the floor allow light to pass to floors below.

A student in the 1970s recounted another strange event. He was spending his study time deep in the Decks at one of the provided desks. The hairs on the back of his neck began to prickle, and he became aware that someone, something, was watching him. He at first tried to ignore it, thinking that someone must be looking for a book or somewhere to sit, but the sensation did not leave him. Finally, he turned to see the shadow of someone at the edge of one of the shelves down the row. Someone was simply standing there, staring at him just beyond his view. He stood up, and the shadow moved, the person apparently taking the hint and moving on. The student, however, was upset over being interrupted and stared at, so he marched after whoever it had been to tell him off. As soon as he came around the corner of the shelf, he found the aisle deserted. Confused, he began running along the rows, looking down each walkway and finding himself utterly alone. The student returned to his desk, packed his things and studied elsewhere for the rest of his academic career.

While the Decks have inexplicable activity, the Great Reading Room is also known for its own events that continue to perplex and even scare students as they attempt to study. Running the length of the old library, the Great Reading Room features huge windows on the east and west, catching natural light to illuminate the room. Wood paneling decorates the edges and ceiling, culminating in rafters that make the room seem to be a cathedral of learning. Wooden angels carry the rafters, each one carved with a unique expression. Hundreds of doctoral dissertations and master's theses from across the decades fill the walls on built-in shelves. The floor is lined with enormous, heavy, wooden tables, with dozens of chairs filled with eager learners.

The Great Reading Room is the quietest place on campus. Despite almost always having busy studiers and even being crowded during final exams to the point of not having a free chair to fill, the room is deathly quiet. Cellphones must be shut off, and anyone who happens to forget is immediately ostracized and even asked to leave upon it ringing. Talking in the Great Reading Room is unheard of. Even coughing too loudly earns glares from fellow students.

While students work diligently at their studies, they sometimes leap up in pain for what appears to be no reason. According to a number of cases, a student will be sitting, poring over a book, almost oblivious to the world. Suddenly, something attacks them with a sharp smack on their wrists or neck. They look up, and nothing is there. No snapped rubber bands as a prank or stern schoolmarm with a ruler in hand—no signs of anything that

The Great Reading Room.

might have bit them or the bite marks it would have left. Instead, students attribute the strange attacks to the library ghost. Even though no one confesses to any wrongdoing on their part, some students suggest that the ghost is ensuring that the Great Reading Room remains a place without casual studiers leaning back in chairs or goofing off in a space needed for more diligent students.

Or perhaps the library ghost simply thinks that they are studying too hard and could use a break.

THE NEVER-ENDING AFFAIR

Memorial Student Union

The Union is known to all students as a great place to hang out, grab a bite to eat, attend club meetings and catch free movies on Friday nights. Ideas for the Union went back as far as 1921, but it was the burning of the local YMCA in 1922 that pushed the notion forward with unstoppable momentum. Housing for students has always been an issue in Norman, and many unmarried young men made their temporary homes at the YMCA that once stood on Campus Corner. Necessity spurred the movement, and fundraising began.

Initial plans called for a combined football stadium/student union as the focus of extracurricular activity on campus, with plans drawn up in 1925. The football stadium had already begun its construction in 1923 with sixteen thousand permanent seats, and Coach Bennie Owen called for two separate structures. The union was bumped northward while construction on expanding the stadium continued. In 1928, the student body voted a $2.50 annual "Union" fee upon itself to support the Union, and construction finally began in 1929. Both the stadium and the Union were named in memory of the students and staff who had died in World War I.

In its construction, the Union was built far larger than it needed to be, showing great expectations for growth. While there were still vast empty spaces for congregating, the Union soon filled with shops, two bowling alleys, a pool hall and the Will Rogers cafeteria, which became Norman's premier spot for after-church lunch on Sundays. Other rooms that would later fill with offices were initially used as boarding rooms, including entire apartments on the third floor where the Union management offices are today.

In the 1950s, one of these apartments was rented by a Norman city official. He and his secretary had fallen into an affair that continued to escalate into carnality and theft. The city rented the apartment as space for meetings and for out-of-town guests, but it was often free for the official and his secretary to meet there and carry on their affair. They took trips together as "business" for the city, taxpayers unknowingly supporting the dishonest relationship.

The two realized that they could not go on as they were forever. It was only a matter of time before they would be suspected, if that had not already started, and they would be eventually caught. In addition to the destruction of a marriage, both of them would go to prison for theft of public funds, compounded by acting together in conspiracy to do so. They decided that they had gone too far with no chance of retribution, so the best they could hope for was to escape with as much public money as they could.

Setting up a way to drain thousands of dollars from the city accounts, they devised a plot to flee to Mexico, where they would start a new life for themselves. They packed up the money and what belongings they could bring without raising too much suspicion, and then they headed south.

The Memorial Student Union.

Being seen crossing the border would leave too much of a trail to follow and perhaps even get the state department involved, a force that could pressure local police far more than the couple could bribe their way out of trouble. They determined that it would be best to sneak across the border.

Illegal travel between the United States and Mexico is not a modern concept. As far back as the settlement of Texas, many of the American pioneers there did not lawfully make their claims on farms and ranches.

Decades later, Mexican rebels such as Pancho Villa would lead raids across the border, striking towns in New Mexico and Texas and leaving dozens dead alongside burned-out buildings. Prompted by the attacks, Americans under General John J. Pershing crossed the border in a semi-legal military operation into northern Mexico. After Mexico became stable, criminal trade and illegal immigration continued to flow back and forth across the border. An entire transportation industry has been built up around the operation, and it was with these traffickers that the couple hoped to find their way across.

A sign showing that the Union is dedicated in memory of students who fought for our freedom.

In a cantina, they began asking if there was someone who could guide them across the border. They offered to pay handsomely, and suspicious eyebrows were raised on how a couple could easily part with so much money. A few men agreed to take them out into the desert for a crossing, and the couple was never seen again. Outside the bounds of law, the two were safe from border officials, but they were also left to the mercy of their guides, who most likely hid the bodies and seized their cases of stolen public money.

Where the couple had their apartment has long been converted into offices. Narrow hallways are lined by rooms filled with desks, humming computers and the many papers required to run the activities of the Memorial Student Union. The office suites are usually bustling with activity, and it is rare that things are quiet. Even summers between semesters bring renovations and visiting groups from off campus. When the offices are quiet, however, strange noises have been heard and movement sensed.

Footsteps are the most frequently heard inexplicable noise. A number of people have worked late and heard footsteps coming down the hallway. The lights, like many on campus, are set to motion sensors that flick on. Even knowing that everyone else has left and the office doors were to have been locked, people hear the steps and see the lights turn on. They get up from their desks to see who is wandering around, but when they peek into the hallway, nothing is found there.

Halls of the Memorial Student Union.

Workers have also made complaints of banging noises from behind closed doors. Despite the office being left and locked by its mortal inhabitants, something is known to make the strange thumping sounds. People at times return to their office and find objects on the desk overturned or papers scattered. Most of the workers have simply gotten used to the problem or purposely do not dwell on it. Many parapsychologists believe that acknowledging the ghost only causes more interaction, and folks in the office agree that the less ghostly activity they have, the better.

The Union jukebox, which often begins playing by itself.

In addition to the offices that were once apartments, the Union's famous jukebox is believed to be haunted. It is original to the 1950s, the time of the heyday of jukeboxes as centers of entertainment. Today, the jukebox rests in the renovated Will Rogers Cafeteria next to a dance floor. Students are still able to pump in coins and listen to music both old and new.

Periodically at night and even during the day, the jukebox will turn itself on and play music unprovoked. Many patrons of the Union agree that the jukebox is old and so must have electronic issues from time to time. However, despite having undergone numerous repairs that should fix such issues, the jukebox continues to surprise people with sudden serenades.

In one case from 1971, when the jukebox was on the second floor, a janitorial services worker attempted to listen to "Superstar" as performed by the Carpenters. Every time he put in his money and punched the code, however, Peter, Paul and Mary's "Leaving on a Jet Plane" would start up. After having this problem for several days and complaining to his co-workers, they decided to open up the jukebox. Without touching any of the electronics controlling the jukebox, they swapped the records so that typing in the code for "Superstar" would follow whatever error the jukebox had and play the slot previously held by "Leaving on a Jet Plane." This time, when they punched the code, "Leaving on a Jet Plane" started again. The workers decided that they would leave the jukebox and whatever cursed it alone.

Some in the Union jokingly suggest that the couple who made their ill-fated attempt at escaping together to Mexico use the jukebox as a lament, wishing that they had flown.

HIGH HEELS

Gittinger Hall

Two buildings of curious architecture stand on the western side of the campus's South Oval. Gittinger and Kaufman form bulky L-shapes that nearly mirror each other. Built in the 1960s as the campus was working to update and expand its classrooms, the new buildings offered space for small classes. Plans called for a large auditorium to join the buildings, but they fell through, and instead the South Oval has its twins housing the English department in one and the modern languages department in another.

Despite serving as the home for the English department, the building is named for Roy Gittinger, one of the great professors of history at the University of Oklahoma. Gittinger himself was an OU alumnus from the class of 1902. Upon Gittinger's graduation, OU president David Ross Boyd hired him to the preparatory department, an ancestor of University College's Freshman Programs. Gittinger became principal of the department, one of more than half a dozen positions he held over fifty years of service to the university. His 1917 book *The Formation of the State of Oklahoma (1803–1906)* served as one of the first academic works about the young state.

In 1942, Gittinger wrote *The University of Oklahoma: A History of Fifty Years 1892–1942*, a history book that must have come easily as he had firsthand knowledge for all but the initial years of the school. He retired from the university in 1950 after half a century at the school. Upon the announcement of his retirement, President George Lynn Cross, the eighth president Gittinger had known, wrote that Gittinger had "made a greater contribution to the University of Oklahoma than any other person in the entire history of the institution." It was determined that the new building on the South Oval finished in 1952 would be named in his honor, even if it were for another department.

In addition to its student body learning the finer details of the essay-writing process in composition and the higher level classes studying literature, Gittinger is home to what some have dubbed "the secretary ghost." Many secretaries have passed through the department over the years, but no one can think of a reason any particular one might return to haunt the building. Others suggest that it may be a former professor, still studying the great works and walking to and fro in the halls.

The ghost is, at least, a coffee lover. On occasions without number, the first-floor lounge has been the site of peculiar paranormal activity involving

Right: The English building, where a ghostly secretary is said to roam.

Below: The echoes of high heels ring on the third floor, despite no one walking.

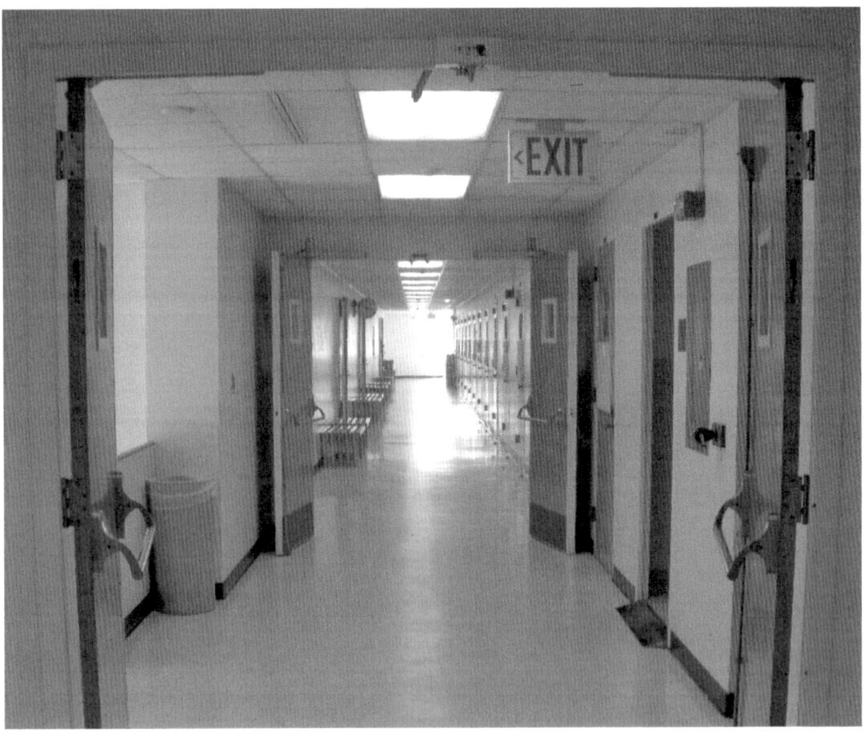

the coffee maker. According to campus stories, even when no one has been around to do so, the machine has been filled with hot water and instant coffee and turned on. In further instances, cups of coffee have even been poured and then left on the counter beside the pot, still warm.

On the third floor, the disembodied sound of high heels walking around has been heard by a number of witnesses. It is not uncommon to hear the *click-clack* of heels in the building, but the sound often rings at night while graduate students are poring over work in their offices. Hearing the ruckus, they look out their door as they expect someone to pass, but no one ever does. The sound then recedes, walking the rest of the way down the corridor. Some have even attempted to follow the sound, but there has been no record of seeing a figure to match the echoing steps.

Also on the third floor is a room that notoriously locks itself. The classroom is no different from any other, yet the door is constantly locked. Signs have been posted warning students not to tamper with the push-button locks on the doors. Tape has even been wrapped tightly over the mechanical locking button, making it difficult to press. Still, students and professors trying to get into the classroom find it locked tight, and perturbed members of the IT office down the hall are routinely asked to unlock it.

No one is sure who this ghost could be with her love of coffee and high-heeled shoes and an attachment to the third floor. The department has had a number of colorful individuals in its past, including a graduate student who determined that her class would appreciate poetry more if she read it in the nude. The spirit of Gittinger remains a mystery.

SHADOWS IN THE WINDOWS

Copeland Hall

The first Journalism Building on campus was completed in 1958 and three years later renamed in honor of Dr. Fayette Copeland, who had served the school for thirty-five years. He had begun his career at OU in 1916 by joining a quartet of journalism students in improving the campus newspaper. It had been semiweekly up to that time, but they sought to increase student output tenfold. The young journalists turned the paper into a daily, printing every morning during school except weekends. The *Oklahoma Daily* continues to follow their example, with the only interruption being 1918 due to paper shortages and support for the war effort during World War I. Copeland was editor of the *Daily* in 1917 and the *Sooner* yearbook in 1919. Copeland soon joined the staff as publicity director and then the faculty as assistant professor of journalism.

Almost every night for the past fifty years, Copeland Hall has been busy with student journalists working on their assignments. While the newspaper office is home to the latest hours during the semester, the summer passes that title to the yearbook office in the back hallway of the first floor. Sped on by energy drinks and coffee, students work to prepare that year's tome commemorating the many events, clubs and personalities on campus. The *Sooner* yearbook has been produced since the first decade of the 1900s, and it grows larger every year.

In the yearbook office, students often joke that the rooms are haunted. Other students who have experienced strange events either join in on the jokes to comfort themselves or consider it no laughing matter. Boisterous poltergeists seem to have taken up residence alongside the busy mortals.

Students working in the office at night, and even during the day, witness weird activity. A pile of paper will be sitting peacefully on a desktop when it

Copeland Hall, the journalism building.

The halls of Copeland, where spirits are said to run rampant.

begins to slide off. Sometimes it might be slow, a few pages at a time, which could be explained by a shift in the flow of air conditioning or perhaps the top pages being slightly off-balance. On other occasions, the entire stack would plummet as if it were batted by an unseen hand.

Papers are not the only things apparently toyed with by the entities. A book might be resting on the shelf comfortably and then suddenly lean back and fall. Chairs and bottles may be found overturned. The window blinds may wave even when the blowers from the heating and air are not active.

Student journalists regularly walk into the office to find it in shambles. Of course, it is easily an issue blamed on workers the night before not cleaning up after themselves. When asked, those workers, even if guilty, blame the ghosts as a way out of trouble. Others genuinely hold that, while the building is dark and locked, ghosts run rampant through the office, knocking over office supplies and generally making a mess. Naysayers scoff, and skeptics say that it is far more likely that the culprits may be found among the living, as college students are rarely known for their tidiness.

Still, there has been visual confirmation of rambunctious ghosts in Copeland Hall. Early one morning as the janitorial services worker was finishing her rounds, she packed her equipment into her vehicle, parked in the small lot adjacent to the building. As she finished, she happened to glance back at the building. Shadows of human forms ran back and forth in front of the windows as if romping through the room.

She called her supervisor to report the shadows, explaining her thought that some students had gotten into the building after hours and saying, "You might want to call security to chase them out."

Her supervisor replied glibly, "It's just the ghosts. Don't worry about it."

She decided not to worry about it and continues to clean up after them to this day.

Unquiet Spirits

Cate Center and the Cafeteria Basement

Cate Center began as the "Women's Quadrangle" in 1948 as the university organized new housing for female students. Coeds had previously lived closer to classroom buildings in Hester Hall, but the rooms were small and ill-equipped for the growing student population. Twelve years after it first began, the network of three-story buildings was renamed the Cate Center after Roscoe Cate, a journalism graduate of the University of Oklahoma who used his business-savvy mind to climb to the position of financial vice-president.

Over more than sixty years, Cate has been home to thousands of young women and, following restructuring of dorm regulations, men. It has also been home to a number of stories of paranormal activity, primarily poltergeists.

German for "noisy ghost," poltergeist activity goes back centuries, accounting for any kind of unseen force causing movement or clamor. Some forces are believed to be malicious, while others are simply playful or attempting to make themselves known. There have been hundreds of documented cases of poltergeists around the world, with formal study dating back as far as 1698 in the *Lithobolia* pamphlet telling of a "stone-throwing ghost" that attacked the Walton family home in New Hampshire for several months. Informal witness goes back to time immemorial.

In the majority of cases of sudden poltergeist activity, it seems to center on adolescent children, usually in their early teens. Some parapsychologists argue that the sexual awakening of these youngsters brings up or attracts paranormal activity. Others argue that noisy spirits are welcomed due to a more psychological nature when households begin to change, often unhappily, as teens grow out of dependent childhood into independent adulthood. In either case, while some consider college students too old to be magnets for poltergeists, it is hard to find a place more filled with newly awakened, confused sexual energy and underlying social turmoil than college dormitories.

There have been a number of rumors and stories about ghosts in all parts of Cate. None of them seem to stay very long, which points to the possibility of poltergeists attaching themselves to particular students or groups of students rather than a formal haunting with a nameable ghost. Skeptics might argue that the cases are isolated and more likely dorm equipment in need of repair or tricks of the imagination. However, there are a number of times when material explanations simply do not satisfy.

Unlike the four-person suite bathrooms of the Towers, Cate Center features large bathrooms at the ends of halls. These are frequented by twelve, twenty and sometimes more students, depending on the hall. With so much activity, it is difficult to imagine a time when it would be quiet enough to notice anything outside the normal noise.

Yet this is the case in a number of different stories. In one bathroom, a young lady stated that the door to the end stall would open itself. The simple argument for such is an imbalance on the hinge, but she explained that even when locked, the door undoes itself and swings open. Out of modesty—and simple eeriness—the end stall was rarely used.

In another case, again in a shared bathroom, a shower turns itself off. Skeptics could easily argue that with so many people using the plumbing, it is bound to come to certain eccentricities. However, rather than the pipe becoming clogged or the pressure falling off, those who witnessed it said that the handle itself turned. A student would be in the shower, scrubbing and enjoying the water when it would suddenly drop off. More than the creepiness of a potential haunting, the girls who used the shower were frustrated by having to turn the water back on to get soap out of their eyes or hair. Like the bathroom stall, the shower quickly became deserted.

Events are not always limited to bathrooms. One student complained of cold gusts and shoves while walking in a particular hallway. He would be walking down the hall when he would feel a sensation similar to the blower on the air conditioning starting up. Sometimes he would feel as if something had brushed past or even shoved him. Coldness is often associated with ghostly activity, and being pinched, poked or grabbed is not uncommon during poltergeist activity. He said that no one else felt the strange commotion or at least that no one would admit it.

The most interesting case of poltergeist activity came from a pair of roommates who had problems hanging posters. Whenever they put something on their west wall, it would fall off. It began with a Beatles poster that they hung up with sticky tack. It fell, so they determined to rehang it with tape. The tape, too, gave way. Finally, they decided to break housing rules and drill into the wall to install hangers for the poster. Not only did the poster fall, but the hangers also came out of the wall. They gave up on the poster, and the wall remained undecorated until they started taping up sheets with assignments as reminders to get their homework done.

The pages would sometimes fall or fly across the room. Rather than the tape coming loose, the paper would jerk itself away from the wall as if it had been grabbed and torn off. If heavier items were placed on the wall, they would be thrown. Pictures of themselves, friends and family were taken down and crumpled. One roommate noted that sometimes things even flew at them, particularly toward their heads. Their solution to the problem was to stop putting things on the wall, which seemed to satisfy whatever it was that took down the posters.

Typically, poltergeists are unnamed as part of the definition of the manifestation. It is simply a force that acts seemingly at random or perhaps with a goal, such as water conservation or keeping a wall clear of decorations. Others hold that a poltergeist may be a once-human spirit interacting with the mortal realm, noisily making itself known.

One such example of a named poltergeist is the spirit believed to dwell in the Cate Cafeteria basement. In the summer of 1986, much as it does today, the university lent out its spare housing and classrooms to summer programs for teens to get a taste of higher learning. The Summer Institute of Linguistics program brought students together to look at languages in a deeper level than typically seen in high school foreign language programs. Thirteen-year-old Dallasite Jonathon Yost was among the summer linguists who came into Cate Cafeteria for lunch on August 5. He got away from his group and sneaked down to play in the basement.

The basement of Cate is a dark, labyrinthine area full of metal, brick and the smell of moisture. Buzzes emanate from the machinery cooling the freezers, the overhead lights and the heavy-duty power lines to run the

Entrance to Cate Center.

various devices upstairs in the kitchen. The ceiling is low, and there is an overall sense of claustrophobia. Even without the rumor of being haunted, it is not a place someone would want to be in long.

Yost found the dumbwaiter, the small elevator used to bring boxes up from the basement to the main floor without lugging them up the stairs. He decided that he would ride the dumbwaiter upstairs, an antic not unreasonable for a thirteen-year-old.

Unfortunately, as Yost climbed into the dumbwaiter, he did not quite get all the way in. Safety measures should have prevented the dumbwaiter from moving when the doors were still open. However, whether through Yost's actions or those of someone in the decades-long history of the building, the safeties had been broken off. A university employee upstairs, not knowing that Yost was playing in the dumbwaiter, pressed the button to call it upstairs. It began to move upward with Yost's head still sticking out. The wall caught his neck, and the strong engine powering the dumbwaiter beheaded him.

Paramedics rushed to the scene, but it was clear that Yost was dead. The faculty and students of the Summer Institute of Linguistics waited anxiously for news while holding hands and praying in the cafeteria just yards away from their lost fellow student. Norman police arrived, and the officer in his report said that it was the worst thing he had ever seen. It took three hours for police and paramedics to free Yost's body from the dumbwaiter. Even though he was taken away and buried, many feel that he is still in the basement, playing.

Housing and Food Services employees do not like going down into the basement, especially at night and never alone. The basement carries the dark vibe that many basements do, but the noises that come from it are notoriously spooky.

Workers in the kitchen above have reported a number of strange sounds. One interviewee said that, as he was setting up to open early one morning, there was a loud bang from the dumbwaiter, as if someone had hit it. He knew that he was the only one there that morning, and he chose to investigate. The noises come even when others are there to hear it. Despite the employees knowing that no one has gone into the basement, they hear clanging noises that sound as if someone is working on machinery or "fixing something."

Another worker said in an interview that the basement freezer is notorious for shutting itself off. Rather than a malfunctioning thermostat or even an electrical failure, the issue is the physical switch on the top of the back of the freezer. To switch it on, a worker has to find a stepstool and climb back to reach it. They blame Jonathon, but they certainly would not vent their frustration at him inside the basement.

The Oklahoma City Ghost Club paranormal investigation team has spent evenings in the kitchen and basement attempting to find hard evidence of ghostly activity. On the team's first visit, a reporter and a photographer from the *Oklahoma Daily* college newspaper went along with them. Rather than "relying on psychic impressions," the investigators attempted to be as scientific as possible with their observations, using equipment such as "a digital camera, audio recording, a night-vision video camera and electromagnetic field detectors," as well as "special low frequency flashlights" that would not interfere with cameras. Skeptics often declare supposed photographic evidence as blurs in the film or show that ghostly "orbs" can very well be reflections from dust particles.

Over the course of its investigations, the Ghost Club's digital cameras did not capture any images of ghostly activity either in stills or video. Members' EMF readers and thermometers did not detect anything out of the normal. One EVP, however, did include a voice that sounded like a child saying, "Get some ice."

Cate Cafeteria, where young Jonathon Yost sneaked away from his group in 1986.

The photographer from the *Daily*, however, had a stroke of luck with a film camera. A picture taken of the dumbwaiter when no outside light was present developed with a strange orange outline of a human body. It is apparently walking toward the camera, its hand outstretched. The hand and the face are especially bright. According to the *Daily*'s report, the image is on the negative as well as the print, ruling out the possibility that the ghostly image is a developing error.

Filmmaker and OU graduate David Burkhart spent another evening in the basement for his final project, entitled *Alone in the Basement*. The documentary short records his early fascination with the afterlife, which became all the more important to him after the passing of his father. He intended originally to spend an entire night down in the basement, but after only a few hours, he had all the evidence he felt he would need. Burkhart said that he did not know whether he had actually had any encounter with a real ghost, but something terrified him to the point that he does not even want to question it.

Jump

Walker Tower

Walker Tower is infamous for its lively history. While Adams Tower to the west predates it by a year and Walker's twin, Couch, is just as old, to quote flabbergasted students, "All the weird stuff happens to Walker!" As an example, an episode of the Learning Channel's *I Didn't Know I Was Pregnant* followed the 2009 story of a freshman who thought that her weight gain had been the "Freshman 15" until her supposed "bad cramps" turned out to be contractions. The baby was born in the suite bathroom shared between two rooms, with her shocked roommate acting as midwife.

The "Towers," as they are known on campus to differentiate them with the shorter halls of Cate Center, were constructed in the mid-1960s as part of the permanent expansion for student accommodation. Temporary and emergency housing had shot up around the campus with the surge of students following the Second World War, and President Cross worked to reorganize the haphazard living space. The new towers went up, and as soon as they were occupied, there seemed to be something strange about Walker.

Walker Tower is notorious for its post-midnight fire alarms. Practical jokes are customary on college campuses across the world, and pulling a fire alarm, while illegal and very dangerous, is one of the most popular ways to prank fellow students as they stumble down the stairs, bedraggled and sleepy. For whatever reason, whether statistical or by some design, Walker Tower holds more false fire alarms than the other housing centers on campus. Pranksters are often caught, but so many have gotten away that some suggest it could be the act of something beyond the physical.

The most famous fire in Walker's history happened in 1971 as part of a rash of violence that swept over campus. On a single night on November 17, four fires broke out on campus, causing as much as $200,000 in damages. The week before, there had been an attempt at fire-bombing the administration building, but it had been stopped by watchful campus security. Vandalism, including widespread use of racial slurs against new black students, covered the campus, especially the Bizzell Memorial Library, where George McLaurin won his 1950 Supreme Court case and the right to use the Great Reading Room alongside white students. The same night as the fires, a bullet smashed through a window of the Black People's Union building.

Walker Tower dormitory.

In addition to fires, Walker is known as the tragic host of two suicidal jumps. On April 4, 1971, freshman Allan Floyd Adkisson was stumbling despondently around the eighth floor. He carried a wine bottle and was believed by a collection of students playing cards in the lounge to be under the influence of drugs. When he tried forcing an elevator door open, they summoned the resident adviser. Before they could calm him down, Adkisson charged one of the windows in the lounge. The plate glass is built into the wall, making opening the windows impossible. It is thick enough that someone accidentally falling would not be in any danger of it breaking. Whether through his determination or use of brain-addling enhancement drugs such as PCP, Adkisson broke through the window and launched himself with such force that his body nearly reached the street from the center of the building before the eight floors of space ran out. In his room, officers found papers that his roommate described as a "Dear John" letter from his girlfriend.

Another jumper, and Walker's most famous, also leaped due to emotional turmoil. On Friday, September 22, 1967, thirty-nine-year-old Frank Green was released from Central State (now Griffin Memorial) Mental Hospital after voluntarily checking himself in the previous Tuesday. He had supper there a little before 6:00 p.m. Later, on foot, he hailed the Checker Cab taxi of Mrs. Lucy Steves, who noted the smell of alcohol on him. Green asked her to drive him to the "New Towers" on campus, as they had not even gotten their official names yet. The fare came to $4.35, but he only had a dollar. On the trip, he said he was going to jump.

Green exited the taxi on Asp, where students still unload their laundry baskets and computers today. He went into the building and rode up the elevator along with Ted Wise, a student from another college who was visiting a friend in the building. Green saw that Wise was getting off at the tenth floor and said, "I'm going on to twelve to jump."

Wise, somewhat shaken, exited the elevator as planned. He told Blaine Stephen, an Oklahoma Highway Patrol recruiter who was staying in the dorm as part of a university program, about the man. Stephen raced upstairs to investigate.

In the meantime, Green had gotten off on the twelfth floor and walked to a window by the lounge. He took a chair and broke out the glass. Green calmly kicked out the remaining glass from the window, brushed

The elevators used by Green in 1967.

clean the concrete ledge beyond and then he stepped outside. The noise caught the attention of people on the sidewalk, and they began gathering below. Word spread quickly, and within minutes, more than two hundred spectators had congregated.

Green sat down on the ledge over one hundred feet in the air. He scooted forward, dangling his feet over the side of the concrete. Students began calling up to Green, asking what he was doing. Green yelled back that he was going to jump.

For whatever reason, the crowd of college students did not take him seriously. They yelled up at him to stop fooling around and go inside. Green refused and replied again that he was going to jump. He even suggested, "You'd better get them women folks out of here." The crowd only rolled its collective eyes.

Whenever someone yelled up loudly enough for him to hear, Green would yell back replies. When challenged about whether he was really going to jump, Green answered, "You're damn right I'm going to jump."

Bob Botswick, a sports publicity student, called up to Green, trying to get his name. Green never replied to him. Instead, Green was busy with the increasingly belligerent crowd. They began telling him that nobody was impressed by his showing off and that he did not really have the guts to jump. Botswick later recalled, "I don't think anyone realized he was up there for real. Some kids were just razzing him and going on like that."

Officer Stephen arrived at the window as the crowd was becoming more and more excited below. He spotted Green easily, sitting on the concrete outside the broken window. Green's hands were covered in blood from the glass, but he did not seem to mind. He was even swinging his feet as he sat twelve stories up.

Stephen moved to stop him, but Green threatened, "I'm going. If you get a hold of me, you're going with me." While Stephen rushed downstairs to get help preventing Green from suicide without endangering his own life, a new cry rang up from the crowd. Somewhere in the midst of two hundred people, someone shouted, chanting, "Jump! Jump!" The rest of the crowd, one by one, started joining in. "Jump! Jump! Jump!" Soon hundreds of voices were calling up to Green, in a joke not one of them understood, "Jump! Jump! Jump! Jump!"

Green took off his outer shirt, folded it and set it beside him. Then he placed his hands on either side of his body on the edge of the concrete. According to witnesses, he calmly "boosted himself up and off the ledge. He did a sort of gentle flip as he came down."

The crowd's mood instantly shifted. A gasp rose out of them, and then everyone was silent as Green fell. As they watched, his body plummeted floor by floor before finally hitting the ground, where, it is said, he bounced six feet back up into the air and then came to a rest on his stomach and left side.

Noise again broke out from the crowd. More gasps and finally screams began. The police arrived, their sirens wailing only barely too late. Stephen returned to the window too late as well, finding the neatly folded outer shirt on the ledge, the words "Frank R. Green" printed in it. The entire ordeal took only three to five minutes according to witnesses, but its climactic end would leave it in their minds forever.

One visitor on a ghost tour stopped after to ask about the Walker Tower poltergeist. According to him, during his tenure at school in the 1970s, the resident adviser's room on the twelfth floor had been haunted by a noisy ghost. After several interviews of advisers in the dorm today, no one was able to confirm the story. Nonetheless, he had been adamant that there had been a presence in that room in his own time. He suggested that it could very well be Frank Green.

Spirits that come from violent ends are often known to linger, seeking out solace to the tragic ends of their lives. Some, such as the visitor on the tour, believe that Green may have hung around the twelfth floor. He did not hold the poltergeist as any malicious entity, instead perhaps looking for attention, as some thought Green was doing in his last minutes of life.

These thoughts go back to the many fire alarms of Walker as well, often blamed on a "ghost" whether out of jest or frustration. Perhaps Green is still shaking up campus for a short while, even after death. There is also the possibility of the ghost being young Allan Adkisson. His spirit, still in agony over a lost love, may be seeking revenge by interrupting the blissful rest of others that he will never know.

Basketball, the Radio and Peeping

The Huff

A common trick to pull on incoming freshmen is to tell them, "Don't shower in the gym. It's haunted!" As humorous as it is to see their bewildered faces, even more bewilderment comes when it is found out that there may be something true about this wild story.

Named for the state regent who masterminded the creation of a top-level conditioning facility for the school, the Huston Huffman Physical Fitness Center began to serve students, faculty and staff in 1981. It is a sprawling facility accessible not only to OU affiliates but also Normanites who wish to exercise. Visitors to the "Huff," as it is called by students in the know, pass by large fitness classrooms on their way to the indoor track, rock wall or weight rooms. An aerobics room consists of dozens of machines lined up like a fat-burning factory. Screens fill the eyes of exercisers, and earbuds plugged into iPods with energizing playlists keep distraction at bay. Beneath these are the courts for basketball, racquetball, table tennis and even badminton.

In researching for the ghost tour, one of the first questions asked is, "Has anyone ever died here?" The reply was a quiet, "We don't like to talk about it." While there have not been any famous deaths in the gym, it is still a place of heavy activity where people can overexert themselves. Whether the spirit believed to be haunting the Huff is a former patron or simply a roaming entity that decided to take up residence, there have been a number of strange events suggesting that something out of the normal is at work.

When closing late at night, all of the exercise equipment is wiped down and put away. Basketballs are put onto their racks, weights are stacked and electronic treadmills are shut down. The workers at the Huff leave it perfectly tucked in and the lights shut off. However, on certain occasions, the janitorial services workers will come in later on to find basketballs scattered around the court as if someone had been playing with them.

The simple explanation is "gym rats." Rather than the furry, four-legged versions, these are exercisers who sneakily stay behind after the staff has shut up the gym. They work out in solitude and perhaps enjoy the thrill of trespassing, raising their adrenaline. As with every facility, the Huff has had its cases of gym rats, but that does not explain the basketballs. Playing basketball with a group of fellow rats would require only one ball, not the several scattered around. It could very well be someone shooting baskets and collecting a fresh ball rather than picking up the old one, but there is the question of the lights.

Like most large spaces, the gym lights are tied into a control panel. The lights for the basketball courts hang far above, two stories up, so that the same lights can be used for the indoor running track. Large windows make any light in the space easily visible from the outside, yet there have not been cases where lights were noticed. Whoever is playing basketball seems to be doing so in the dark. A creative skeptic might argue about personal headlights or even night-vision goggles, but that seems like a great deal of trouble simply to play basketball.

While the basketballs may not be altogether convincing, another strange instance, concerning the gym-wide radio, hints at paranormal activity. Again, all of the equipment is shut down as the staff leaves for the night. Janitorial services come in to empty wastebaskets and mop, for which they turn on lights, but they shut them down as they leave. When the early shift comes in, among its opening duties is to start up everything. Sometimes, however, the first person to unlock the door finds the gym filled with music. A radio in the gym office gives the gift of bouncy songs to workers and patrons alike, keeping up the high-paced, excited environment commonly felt in gyms.

Some believe that the gym ghost enjoys it as well. Not only does he like the radio, but he also likes it *loud*. On the occasions when the radio has turned itself on, it also turns itself all the way up. Staff members who have experienced the radio phenomenon describe it as "blaring." It is set to popular music stations, country and rock, as the taste of any Sooner, but the music is far louder than anyone could stand in the office. Workers are quick to turn it down, and there does not seem to be any reciprocity from whatever cranked the radio. Skeptics quickly point out that a blaring radio could easily be a prank pulled by janitorial staff or even an early worker, but there is another instance in the ladies' locker room that anyone has yet to explain.

The locker rooms for the gym are downstairs, tucked away beyond the flashy exercise equipment. Visitors reach them by going underneath the entry into a long, gray hallway. The locker rooms for such a large facility are also large yet somewhat crowded with the rows of benches and storage lockers. There are no windows due to being underground and for privacy's sake, and the low ceiling gives the impression of something like a cave. Behind the lockers and changing areas, there are communal showers.

According to patrons to the ladies' locker room, one corner of the showers always has its light either flickering or burned out completely. Any water-damage issue would affect the other lights, but those are fine. Electricians routinely replace the bulb and check the wiring, but the cause seems to continue despite no material issues. Parapsychologists note that ghosts often affect electric devices. While ghosts do not have physical bodies, fluctuations in electromagnetic fields are believed to be interactions with the spiritual plane. A spirit hiding in the corner of the ladies' shower might very well be causing fluxes that interfere with the light.

Those daring enough to shower in that corner note that it seems colder than the rest of the room. It is no trick of air conditioning as the showers share ventilation, making the cold corner inexplicable. Simply out of the discomfort of the corner, few people are willing to use it, ghost or not. Those who do use it have not reported any sensations of being touched or attacked.

Of course, few are willing to test the eerie corner and prefer to wait for another shower head or just go home.

Part II
Greek Afterlife

Greeks have been a part of Norman society since almost the beginning of the university. Academic and interest clubs grew up in the 1890s as students organized themselves. Those fascinated by archaeology, for example, came together to form clubs in which they could discuss research and even pool resources to launch expeditions, beginning many of the first dig sites for ancient Native American study. Clubs started up around topics ranging from choirs to pharmacy, literature, engineering, languages, zoology and law.

Social fraternal organizations soon followed the clubs, giving students not only a connection on interests but simply through activities as well. Students would gain "brothers" and "sisters" among their classmates with whom they could study, live and network later in life. The frats enjoyed successful early days, and they found their heyday in the Roaring Twenties as America came of age. Colleges became packed with newly wealthy students whose parents could finally afford chances of improvement. Enrollment boosted, and college became a wild place to be as students strutted in their fur coats, rubber shoes and long necklaces. With the newfound energy on campus, fraternal organizations exploded, welcoming many new members as well as new chapters starting up from national organizations. They were dubbed "Greeks," as the cryptic organization names carried initials from the Greek alphabet. Students who did not participate in Greek society were nicknamed "Barbarians," a term rarely used today. When used, both then and now, it is typically derogatory.

Greeks continue to be a major part of college life in Norman. Their enormous houses with dozens of bedrooms, as beautiful as mansions, line the west side of campus for blocks. One-third of the OU population is Greek, giving it a large say in campus goings-on, especially as Greeks are energetically invested in college society. They wear T-shirts emblazoned with their fraternity or sorority's letters, spend sleepless nights assembling homecoming floats and have preplanned events nearly every weekend.

Greek life is a fast-paced one, and in many cases, it seems to continue even after death.

The Exorcism

Old Delta Delta Delta House

In 1973, at the corner of Elm and Brooks, an exorcism took place to rid a violent spirit from a boardinghouse that had once belonged to one of the most famous sororities on campus. The Theta Gamma chapter of the Delta Delta Delta sorority was chartered at the university in 1910, twenty-two years after four ladies at Boston University founded the organization as the first intended to be expanded nationally. Tri-Delts plotted a national government even when having only a handful of chapters, keeping a meticulous written history and contacts with its alumnae. They adopted as their symbols the pearl, the pine tree and the pansy, all figures of growth.

Delta Delta Delta came to the University of Oklahoma through pioneering visitations, one of the first attempts at campaigning from the outside to open a chapter on a new campus rather than a fraternal organization starting itself up and then applying for membership. Over the next century, the OU Tri-Delts grew into one of the most notable groups on campus, always being well represented on the OU Cheer and Pom squads, as well as in pageants and student government. In 1926, after renting houses for their sisters to live in, they were able to buy the house at 700 Elm Avenue, just across the street from the campus and cater-corner to the school's infirmary, Ellison Hall. The Tri-Delts lived there thirty years before building their new house in 1955 farther south on College Street.

The house was sold to the Delta Kappa Epsilon fraternity, which later sold it to a private interest that used it as a boardinghouse. The university bought the house and turned it into the Jim Thorpe Multicultural Center, a place for cultural clubs to meet and have offices, such as the Native American Student Association. It became the place on campus to listen to Taiko drum practice on Tuesday evenings or drop by for pho on Korean Night. Students and faculty advisers alike remarked on the "weird vibe" that the building carried, and rumors spread about its being haunted. In 2009, Jim Thorpe was moved southward, and the building was torn down to make room for the new Zarrow Hall to house the Social Service program.

Many who remember the old Tri-Delta house are shocked, yet not surprised, to find that it once was the site of an exorcism. According to an article from *The Oklahoman*, the ghostly activity began in the early hours of the morning on Sunday, September 16, 1973. The building was undergoing repairs, and its electricity had been shut off until the following Thursday, meaning many of the boarders had gone elsewhere in the time being. A student the article named "Jack" (as he did not want to be associated with the case afterward) stayed in his room on the second floor, using candles for light until going to sleep.

At about one in the morning, Jack woke up choking. "Choking ghosts" are fairly common in the history of parapsychology, although many of the cases are related to sleep apnea—victims roll over in their sleep and close up their windpipes. Before that modern explanation, people routinely blamed ghosts for their interrupted nights.

In Jack's case, the terror only began with choking. He cleared his throat and then lay awake. He heard a harsh gust or breath, something like a gasp. A voice whispered, "No." Another gasp followed. Jack was petrified. He yelled out into the night, "Get out!"

Footsteps began sounding against the old wooden floor next to his bed. They walked away from him, growing softer and then ending altogether. He spent the rest of the night in the room, fearful but not willing to give up.

On Tuesday night, he came back to his room about 12:45 a.m., not necessarily a late hour given the college lifestyle. Jack had left candles burning as a light, but they had gone out. In the pitch-black room, he made his way about halfway across when something unseen grabbed him by the neck. It squeezed like a rope, and he was unable to breathe.

The force threw him down to the floor and continued to throttle him. Jack finally managed to choke out, "Jesus, help me," and whatever it was suddenly let him go. Jack jumped up and ran out the door, not stopping to catch his breath until he reached the front lawn. He decided that he wouldn't sleep in the room again, but he thought that he should at least lock up the room to ensure that no one else got in there.

As soon as Jack touched the door, the footsteps against the wooden floor began to sound again. They were loud, stomping and coming directly toward him. Jack slammed the door shut, locked it and stayed with a friend that night.

Jack was put into contact with Charles Rhoades, the director of the New Age Center of Oklahoma City, through a mutual friend. Rhoades was a medium, able to put himself into trances that allowed him to see beyond the veil of the physical and communicate with spirits. That Saturday, Rhoades led Jack back to the house, along with a reporter from *The Oklahoman* and several other men for support.

They went into the house and down to the basement, where four gravestones rested in a closet. Jack showed the guests the stones, which dated back to the 1890s, and said that they and two others had been brought there as a prank when the house was a fraternity. A police raid discovered the stones, and the two were returned to their rightful sites. The other four were so old that no one knew where they went. So, they remained in the basement, causing onlookers to wonder if any spirit had come to the house searching for its rightful marker.

While the basement gave strange vibes, there was nothing that was willing to communicate with them there. Rhoades set off through the house searching for a "cold spot." According to parapsychology, even ghosts must obey the First Law of Thermodynamics. They use energy to make sounds, move objects or have any interaction with the material realm; therefore, they must also take in energy to maintain conservation. Ghosts do not eat, but they are believed to be able to absorb heat from the mortal world, making a cool breeze or a corner of the room that is inexplicably colder than another candidate for a space that ghosts might inhabit.

The searchers found a cold spot in the hall on the third floor. There, Rhoades sat down and put himself into a trance. After a moment, he told the others, "There are four entities on the floor. All male. One seems more active than the others, more willing to talk to me."

Rhoades began speaking with the ghost and translating his unheard message to the others. The ghost stated that his name was Carl. He was a wandering spirit who had come to the house eight years ago and decided to stay. Carl said that he had not harmed anyone and did not ever wish to do so. He spoke for the other entities on the floor, who also agreed that they wanted no trouble with anybody.

The ghosts left them, and Rhoades came out of his trance. He stood and suggested that they try Jack's room on the second floor, where the violent business had begun. They traipsed down the stairs and huddled into Jack's room, which was small for six people. Rhoades went into another trance and began describing a new spirit.

"I see a little blonde-headed gal. She says her name is Nadine. The last name, I think, is Bolding. She says she was killed in an auto accident in Norman in about 1938. She tells me this used to be her room. She resents anyone intruding." Nadine's spirit had returned to the house, the Tri-Delta sorority at the time, where she considered home.

Rhoades continued, saying that it wasn't just Nadine. "I asked her if there were more entities here. She said, 'There are many of us in the basement.'" One of the ghosts, "Fred," helped her scare away people she doesn't want in her room. Fred acted as her muscle, attacking anyone whom Nadine did not like. In Jack's first choking experience, it seemed Nadine was intimidated by Fred's attack. By that Tuesday, however, she seemed willing to let Fred do anything he wanted to rid Jack from her room.

Rhoades explained that being in the room was unhealthy, not only for the people she attacked but also for herself. She should have gone into the light, the next realm of human existence. If she had any unfinished business, Rhoades volunteered to try to help. Nadine refused the offer and said that it was her room and that she had no interest in leaving it.

Because she and Fred were causing harm to others, Rhoades told her that he could "ask her to leave," meaning, perform an exorcism. Nadine became agitated, and Rhoades affirmed that he would make her leave. Nadine replied, "If you do, I'll tear your heart out." She began talking about ghosts in the basement, including "one mean one…he belongs in a mental hospital." Nadine said that they should wait until dark and that she would get them.

Rhoades suggested not waiting. He sat on the floor silently, with his eyes closed, for a few minutes. Without a word, he stood, stretched and yawned. Then he led the men in joining their hands and reciting a prayer, calling on the name of God to cleanse the house.

He patted Jack on the shoulder and assured him that the spirits were gone. As a precaution, he said not to dwell on the spirits, lest his mind form a window that might bring them back to the mortal realm. Giving ghosts attention seems to cause them to act out further. Over the years, the exorcism was all but forgotten, and the building at 700 Elm was again simply rumored to be haunted.

The *Sooner* yearbook gives a section of its pages each year to group photos of the Greek houses on campus. In Tri-Delta photos of the 1936 and 1937 (but not 1938 or 1939), there is a little blonde gal named Naydene Bowles (also spelled "Nadine") from Tyler, Texas, who had come to OU and joined Delta Delta Delta in the midst of the Great Depression. The reason for her disappearance from the photos is unknown to today's alumnae association of Tri-Delta. Could it be that she had perished in an automobile accident and come back to her room at the sorority house? Anyone glancing at the yearbook could certainly think so.

However, Naydene did not die in 1938. She attended OU and then returned to Tyler, where she married Jim Daniel in 1940. They lived a long life together, with Jim as an oil man and Naydene active in charity work. Mrs. Daniel passed away on August 13, 2012, some seventy-four years after "Nadine" was supposed to have become a ghost.

Another famous exorcism also took place in 1973 on the silver screen. The film *The Exorcist* was released on December 26, 1973, three months *after* the exorcism of the Tri-Delta house, but previews and advertisements would have already placed it in the public mind. Some on campus wonder whether the article is a grand hoax, perhaps orchestrated by the author as a prank or by Rhoades as a publicity stunt for his New Age Center. The notion gains more ground that the instigator simply flipped through the yearbook to pick a victim—beside each young woman's photo was a little poem. The one alongside Naydene's picture read, "Nadine strolls dreamily up the stairs after bidding Jack a fond goodnight."

If a hoax, it is a well-implemented one with a spooky house and a fair bit of research to create a believable story. On the other hand, the choking ghost is not the only case of paranormal activity in the old Tri-Delta house. According to campus legend, the actual ghost was that of a different girl, one who had committed suicide there in the early 1950s. Her spirit haunted the house, and that was the real reason the Deltas moved to their new house. Tri-Delt alumnae to this day say that the building was creepy, although they don't give any reason for it to be haunted.

One evening, the adviser for the Native American Student Association was sitting in his office in a room on the second floor. Business hours were over, and the then Jim Thorpe Multicultural Center was deserted except for him. Down the hall, he heard footsteps walking toward the open door of his office. It was nothing out of the ordinary; the old wooden floors of the building give an alarm to any approaching visitor. The footsteps came up the hall to the door next to his. He waited for the guest to appear. No one did.

After a moment, he called out, "Hello?" No one answered. He got up and went to see who was so shy about coming into his office. When he looked in the hall, not a soul was in it. He was certain that he had heard someone come toward him, and no one could have sneaked away with the creaky floors, yet no one was there. He soon changed offices to a different building on campus.

On a separate occasion in 2003, the Native American Student Association (NASA) lost one of its ceremonial drums. Members searched all through the storage rooms without luck. Someone mentioned checking the basement, but others scoffed at the idea. There was only one set of keys, which the adviser had locked away, and he had certainly not taken the valuable drum into the musty basement. Soon after, the staff came to the house to find it sweltering. Upon entering the basement, they found a broken pipe blowing steam onto the missing drum. It was ruined, and no one could account for how it got into the basement. Following Native American custom, the students buried the once-sacred drum.

When it was decided to tear down the building at 700 Elm, the NASA students decided that they wanted to spend the night in the haunted house. They had great success making a Halloween house for charity, and the spookiness of the season prompted them to ask for one last chance at some scary fun. The adviser agreed but assured them that he wouldn't be staying the night.

After hours of talking and games on the first floor, at about three o'clock in the morning, the students heard footsteps upstairs. They prompted their president (also the biggest of them all) to go up to investigate. He said that he recalled going up the stairs to the third floor, hearing a noise behind a door and opening it up. The next thing he remembers is being back on the couch on the first floor, shaken by his friends, who asked, "What happened?"

They knew more than he did. During his ten-minute blackout, the other students who were huddled on the first floor heard nothing but the door opening at first. After a moment, the president began yelling, "Get out!" and "You're not welcome here!" Something else began to yell back at him in a language they couldn't understand. The voice grew louder, shouting over the president's words. It was clear that this wasn't some kind of performance to prank them.

Then they heard a fight break out. Something heavy hit the floor. Pained shouts and thuds rang down from above. The students dashed upstairs to see what was going on. They found the president on the floor alone. Not waiting to find out what had knocked him down, they picked him up and scurried down to the first floor, where he eventually began to respond to their questions. His left side, left arm and face were covered with scratches.

Although they did not dare to go back up to the third floor, the students stayed in the house the rest of the night as planned. The president's sister later told him that she awoke early, about six o'clock that morning, and saw something sitting at the edge of the mat where he slept. She said it looked just like him, except it had no face. The figure did not seem to frighten her outside of the shock that it was there, and she soon fell back asleep. Some said that it was the president's spirit-double watching over him and protecting him as he slept to ensure whatever had attacked him would not come back.

While there is room for skepticism in all of the paranormal goings-on, few on campus miss the old building.

Fallen Sister

Chi Omega Sorority House

In 1972, the drinking age had not yet been raised to twenty-one, and there were a number of bars on Campus Corner that served all classes of students. On the night of February 6, Nancy Colvert, a member of the Chi Omega sorority, and her boyfriend, Lavoy Ellsworth Jr., of the Beta Theta Pi fraternity, went out to a party. They came back to Ellsworth's room on the third floor of the Beta house. At about 2:30 a.m., Nancy fell ill and rushed to the hallway window, vomiting. While heaving, she lost her balance and fell the thirty feet to the sidewalk below. She was killed instantly, her body wrecked with a fractured skull, fractured wrist and scrapes along her left side.

Alcohol was clearly involved in the incident. The police chief of Norman, Bill Henslee, noted that it was in her bloodstream, but they did not know how much. The Beta president was awakened to talk with the press, which arrived soon after the police, but he knew almost nothing about the accident. He stated, "Everyone is just sick about the whole thing," and said that the house was worried for her parents. Dr. J.R. Morris, vice-president of the university, however, noted that students of the opposite gender were not to visit the rooms after 2:00 a.m. on weekends. In light of the tragedy, however, half an hour of rule-bending seemed nitpicking.

Nancy had been a senior, just months away from graduation. She was an honors student, a swimming instructor at the Campfire Girls Camp

Chi Omega Sorority, where Nancy is said still to dwell.

Cimarron four years running and an active voice on campus. Now her life had been cut short, and the student body held candlelight vigils and wore black armbands for some weeks in mourning of her.

While the official report labeled the incident as an accident prompted by the sudden need to vomit too much alcohol, different versions of the story began to circulate around campus. Rather than a party, it was said that Nancy and Lavoy had gone up to the Blue Onion, a bar featuring live music on Campus Corner in the 1970s. They drank quite a bit before a lover's quarrel began, believed to be Nancy questioning Lavoy's dedication to her while his attention seemed to follow other girls. Lavoy announced that he had had enough and stumbled back to the Beta house, where he went up to his room, locked the door and collapsed into bed.

A little while later, Nancy came up after him. She knocked on his door and called out softly, "Lavoy? It's Nancy." He didn't answer.

Across the hall, a couple of Betas were sitting up, playing cards. Nancy asked if Lavoy had come home, and they replied that he was in his room. Nancy turned back to the door and knocked again, louder this time. She explained that they needed to talk. Lavoy, passed out from a busy night, still didn't answer.

Nancy's alcohol-addled mind began trying to figure out how Lavoy couldn't hear her, and finally she determined that he was ignoring her. She began screaming at Lavoy and pounding on the door. It refused to give. Nancy stood back and shouted, "If you don't open this door right now, I'm going to throw myself out the window!"

Lavoy, of course, didn't hear her and didn't open the door. Nancy was true to her word. Down the hall was the window that now leads to a fire escape. At the time, it simply led into the open air, thirty feet down to the concrete sidewalk below. She jumped, and Lavoy did not wake up until Betas and the police came to question him.

A more sinister version of the story circulated in which Nancy threatened to jump but was pushed instead. She shouted her warning and went to the window but did not go out herself. Rather, the Betas across the hall had grown fed up with her dramatic act and helped her out, ridding themselves and poor Lavoy of a shrill millstone around their necks. It is a harsh rumor and hardly believable, judging from the lack of bruising that would have come from a tussle.

Rather, the story of Nancy's fall seems to be accidental. She had imbibed more alcohol than her system could handle, and the night turned to tragedy. However, Nancy is still believed to persist on campus, haunting both the Beta house and her own sorority next door.

One of the many Nancy stories includes her borrowing fellow sisters' clothes. A Chi-O in the mid-2000s noted how she kept coming into the room to find her dresser drawers open and her clothes ruffled as if someone had been going through them. She first spoke with her roommate, asking, "Why are you digging in my dresser?"

The roommate did not know anything about the dresser; she had thought the other Chi-O was simply a slobby roommate. They put their heads together and reasoned that the building was old, so maybe the dresser was set at a weird angle along the floor. The drawers might slide open under their own weight, and such friction would cause the clothes to become disheveled. They began taping the drawers closed to solve the problem.

Still the dresser popped open. They were dumbfounded and even attempted to move the dresser to another part of the room. After weeks of the strange happenings, someone mentioned Nancy, who was said to still haunt the house. The Chi-O took the suggestion and went back to her room. Somewhat embarrassed, she said aloud, "Nancy? Would you please stop opening my dresser?" The drawers never moved again.

Chi Omega at night.

The best Nancy story comes from the early 1990s, when OU struggled with attacks from rapists and predators. Since that time, lighting along sidewalks and in parking lots has been improved, blue-lit emergency phones with direct lines to campus police were installed and several organizations such as SafeWALK have begun providing volunteers to anyone who would like company crossing campus or to their homes. At the time, however, a number of coeds were threatened with weapons or simply abducted from unsafe corners of the campus.

Not even homes were safe. Before Chi Omega had its electronic lock installed it had a simple mechanical lock. One night, a man was able to pick the lock and sneak inside. He made his way up to the second floor, where the girls' rooms are. None of the upper doors have locks because "why would a sister lock a door against a sister?"

Yet, that night, someone, somehow, had seemingly locked every room on the second floor. The prowler picked a door, anticipated finding a hapless girl to do with as he may, and instead was met by a door being firmly shut as if someone were holding it from the other side. He tried several doors with the same outcome. Eventually, the commotion roused the suspicion of those who were still awake. The police were called, and the man was apprehended, baffled at how he had been so close yet thwarted.

Meanwhile, the girls confusedly wondered what had kept the prowler from attacking them. No one confessed to locking the doors, so they thought of the sister who was neither gone nor forgotten. They agreed that Nancy was looking out for her sisters that night and that she continues to be a protective spirit to this day.

The Back Stairs

Delta Gamma Sorority House

The Delta Gamma Sorority is one of the oldest female fraternal orders in North America, founded in 1873 at the Lewis School for Girls in Oxford, Mississippi. It grew quickly from there, and in 1902 in Boston, it helped form the National Panhellenic Conference to bolster communication and fellowship among sororities alongside Delta Delta Delta and five others. Delta Gamma sisters support in their philanthropy the charity Service for Sight, a tradition continued since 1936 when a DG named Ruth Billow from the chapter in Akron, Ohio, called attention to the needs she knew firsthand following a childhood accident that left her blind. Their motto is simply, "Do good."

Among Delta Gamma's many symbols is their mascot, the Hannah doll. According to DG history, the mascot began with the Vaudeville song "Hannah from Indiana," written by R.H. Wilson, whose daughter would become a DG. Delta Gammas wrote their own song in the 1930s ("Hannah"), and two decades later, they created a doll to serve as a representation for the lyrics. The rag doll featured blonde pigtails, a sailor's uniform with a short skirt and stockings and a hat featuring the Greek letters delta and gamma. Most important is her red heart stitched over her chest. Copies spread throughout the organization, but they could not keep up with demand and were soon replaced by the familiar redheaded Raggedy Ann, who was renamed Hannah. In the modern era, Hannah has even achieved her own Pinterest page, which explains that "Hannah is the ideal DG sister! She is caring and quiet; she'll listen to all of your problems; she'll give you a hug when you need it most!"

At the University of Oklahoma, Hannah has gone beyond doll form into a spirit unto herself. Hannah is believed to be a ghost that has inhabited the

Delta Gamma Sorority House.

house, not due to any death of a mortal but because she was brought to life through the joined power of sisterhood. In 2012, she even began a Twitter account through which she relays messages to DGs and posts thoughts.

Hannah is the excuse for pulling pranks such as suddenly turning out the lights or making anonymous gestures, such as birthday presents marked "From Hannah." When appliances break down or are left particularly dirty, Hannah is blamed. She makes for an excellent scapegoat, as well as good reason for sneaking into other girls' rooms to make scary noises.

Yet there have been strange cases of potential paranormal activity in the house, particularly with doors that open by themselves. The basement door may be closed and latched, yet sisters will turn around to find it slightly ajar. DGs nervously remind one another, "Oh, it's Hannah," and try not to think of what else might be lurking in the house.

Hannah is most notorious at haunting the back stairs. While the front formal staircase to the house is wide open, the back stairs are smaller and used for quick entry to the rooms for girls coming in from the parking lot behind the house. Sisters are warned not to tarry on the stairs, as

Hannah is liable to chase, pinching their legs if she catches them. This may be another excuse to prank one another, particularly rushes, by "goosing" them and causing them to sprint up the stairs. Still, there have been a number of claims by girls stating they were pinched despite being the only person on the stairs.

Parapsychologists often suggest that calling on ghosts or attempting to interact with them can bring about increased ghostly activity. They state that one of the best ways to deal with harmful spirits initially is to simply ignore them and give no sign of interaction. Looking for ghosts and attracting their attention can invite them in. As Delta Gamma sisters continue to name Hannah and even play with Ouija boards attempting to contact her, there may have been a spirit willing to step in and play a role once imaginary. While Hannah and her DGs seem to all be in good fun, the spirit in the AOPi house down the street is anything but fun.

FROM MYTH TO TRUTH

Alpha Omicron Pi Sorority House

Every sorority has enigmatic rituals for its initiates. While hazing is inappropriate for social activities, there are chances to have mutually agreed-on fun, such as telling ghost stories. Older AOPi sisters, along with members of their brother-fraternity Alpha Tau Omega, tell a tale about when the house belonging to the AOPis was once home to ill-fated ATOs. According to the story, there was once a fire in the 1970s so horrible that it nearly destroyed the house. All of the ATOs escaped but one, the one who had accidentally started the fire, and his spirit remains in the house to this day. He haunts certain rooms on the second floor, angry and violent because of his early and awful end. Some of these rooms are locked up and only used for storage. Other rooms are where initiates will sleep.

The older sisters tell their tales of survival, testing their wills against the lost fraternity brother. He is known for tearing jewelry hung up as decorations off the wall and flinging it at sisters. He also breaks thermostats, cranking up the heat or cold to miserable temperatures. One girl tells the story of how she and her roommate woke up in the middle of their first night in the house to their alarm clock beeping and the television showing white static. Nothing had been plugged in yet.

"Bob," as the girls named the ghost, doesn't just stay in the rooms on the second floor. He also prowls the kitchen, banging pots and knocking over anything left out. The girls were warned never to go into the kitchen at night, as he had been known to throw things like loaves of bread and knives. Some of the sisters said they had done research, and it turned out that the brother had really been named "Robert," as if he were trying to tell them his name.

It makes for a great spooky story, but there is no record in newspaper archives of a deadly fire at the house at 1411 Elm. About the time of the supposed fire, there was an actual fire at the Alpha Tau Omega house in Austin, but no one was killed there, either. A fire one week earlier had unfortunately killed a member of the sorority Lambda Chi Alpha on the University of Texas's campus—perhaps the grounds for the story. Norman saw its own fraternity fire in 1980 at the Sigma Chi house, where a new initiate was badly injured but survived.

As with the Delta Gamma house, some believe that talking about a ghost or pretending one is there can invite in a force to impersonate it. While "Hannah" is at most mischievous, the AOPi ghost is rumored to be malicious and violent. According to some, "Bob" is real, and he has freaked out a number of sisters.

One girl began losing sleep, terrified to close her eyes after a white image began appearing in her mirror. At first, it might simply be seen as a reflection of distant lights, but then something began calling her name. She tried to ignore it, but the thing in the mirror and the sound of her name continued to wreck her sleep.

The girl told her sisters about it, which made them giggle nervously at a good ghost story. Then it began happening to them. Girls would wake up frozen in bed, unable to move and unable to scream for help. One said that it felt like something was holding her there, pressing on her. When it finally let go, she glanced up at the clock, which read 3:30 a.m. every time it happened. She took it as a bad dream or waking up partially asleep with the body's motor functions still suspended. When she heard another girl relay the same story, also mentioning 3:30 a.m. without her telling anyone about it, she began to think otherwise.

Strange problems continued to occur during the day as well in the two girls' rooms. A door to a room began slamming itself shut, even when a doorstop was put in place. One girl woke up several nights to find that her small bedroom-sized fridge had been unplugged over and over. Light bulbs would loudly pop and go dead rather than burning out.

Several of the girls grew concerned and approached the housemother for advice. She replied that things like these happenings had occurred time and time again. Her suggestion was to avoid it or ignore it as best as they could.

Parapsychologists seem to agree. The spirit did not seem to do any actual harm other than from the annoyance of missed sleep and replacing light bulbs. Had it been truly malevolent, there may have been a need for action, but as it went, the spirit seemed to be a poltergeist. And yet it knew their names.

A Peculiar Past

Kirkpatrick Manor

The large house at the corner of Cruce and Lahoma has had a long and varied life. It was constructed in 1930 to house the Pi Kappa Phi fraternity with some twenty bedrooms and ten thousand feet of living space. The fraternity soon moved, selling the house to the Pi Beta Phi sorority. In the 1950s, the sorority sold the building to the Presbyterian Homes, Incorporated, an organization that turned the house into a retirement home for women with needs and renamed the house Kirkpatrick Manor in honor of its benefactor. It later changed hands to the Communityworks charity for troubled girls. In 2000, the house was sold to the Triangle fraternity, which began a million-dollar renovation project.

Triangle, a fraternity for "hard" studies, began in 1907 as an organization for students in the fields of science, architecture and engineering. It came to OU in the 1970s, beginning as a club and gaining a charter in 1979 as an official fraternity. The organization is built up to help those some might consider "left-brained" (or "nerds") socialize and build a character that will impress a job interviewer alongside their academic achievements and résumé. The house is noted for being loaded down with computers in various states of repair, all imaginable video game consoles, a free lending library and engineering projects such as recumbent bicycles and solar cell energy plants.

Visitors to Triangle are greeted with a proud tour of the newly remodeled house, which had wood paneling installed and was painted crisp white over the tarnished murals of its older days. Other facets of the tour are equally striking, but not in a positive sense. When the

Triangle Fraternity House.

fraternity moved in, they found an extra room in the basement originally believed to be a simple closet.

At first glance, the room looks normal enough, but little details paint a horrifying picture. The light switch to the overhanging bulb is outside the room. One may easily dismiss that point as simply a different plan in the wiring of the basement so that people can switch the lights on before going in.

The door also has its lock on the outside. Rather than the lock intending to keep people out, it seems to be designed to keep people *in*. The room inside is a simple concrete safe room, similar to a closet, except that an industrial drain rests in the floor. Only rumors and guesses can imagine what the room was used for, and most of them paint pictures of unfair punishments locked in a dark room or even torture. The room is used for storage now, with the lock removed, although the ominous drain is still there.

The explanation for the room ties into history of the house once populated by wayward girls. One girl, it is said, still roams the first floor of the expansive frat. She is described as a plain-looking little girl, perhaps eight to eleven or even younger, wearing a simple dress. People studying in the dining room or sitting in the lounge see her out of the corners of their eyes or simply have the increasing feeling of being watched. When they spin around to see who it is, the figure is gone.

The girl also appears through windows. People outside see her walking through the dining room or standing in the kitchen or lounge. Those who have not heard the stories of the girl wonder if she is someone's sister. By the time they get into the house, she's gone, and everyone inside says that they did not see any little girl. Others glimpse the girl through a window and rush inside hoping to catch her, but she has usually vanished before they are able to get there.

One Triangle was actually able to follow the girl. While sitting on a couch in the lounge, he spotted her walking away from him. He carefully and slowly got up and walked after her through the entry hall, through the dining room and into the kitchen. She slipped through the partially open pantry and into the shadows. He swung the door wide open and found no one inside. There was no sign of any girl but the lingering sensation of a presence there with him.

Paranormal activity also seems to take place on the third floor. Rooms there are often empty as residents choose to live on the second floor and thus have fewer stairs to climb every day. Others prefer the third floor for its quiet atmosphere and less crowded bathroom. There are also those who choose the second floor not out of convenience but out of refusal to sleep on the third floor. Numerous guests and residents alike mention a vibe of creepiness throughout the floor.

No specific stories about the origin of the strange feeling have been verified. It is generally agreed that, as the house served as a retirement home for nearly fifty years, many people must have died there. Residents feel that some of the souls may have stayed behind.

In his room on the third floor, one Triangle slept soundly in his bed until he woke up unable to breathe. Something heavy was sitting on his chest and choking him, but he could not see or feel anything in the dark. He attempted to struggle, but whatever it was refused to let him go. A voice out of the darkness told him, "Nothing will harm you," and then the weight left him. He sat up in his bed and looked for anyone who could have attacked him. The room was empty. He stayed sitting up in his bed until dawn, unable to do anything else.

In another case on the third floor, a different Triangle was asleep when he awoke to the feeling that someone was in the room with him. He sleepily searched the room and found a figure, described as a man, standing beside the door and watching him. The Triangle thought it was someone from the fraternity, so he yelled for it to get out. The figure stood there a while longer and then vanished.

Shocked at the disappearance, he burst from his bed and checked the door. It was still locked from the inside, as it had been since he had gone to bed. The Triangle decided that he did not need the bedroom after all and spent the rest of his time at the house sleeping on couches in the lounge and basement.

The house itself has unsettled spirits, but there is another spot on campus even more famous for its disquiet. On a lonely bench on October 1, 2005, at 7:30 p.m. on a Saturday, while tens of thousands of fans watched the OU football team play its second quarter against Kansas State in the stadium less than a block away, a bomb went off.

People in the stands give different accounts on whether they heard the blast or not. In most interviews, they had not heard anything and did not know about any problem until security shut down several exits before fans left the game. Other interviewees said that they heard a blast

The bench replacing the old one in front of the GL Cross Building.

but just thought it was the Roughneck male cheerleading squad firing blanks from pep rifles. Still others say that the blast was clearly audible even over the roaring crowd and that a small pillar of smoke was visible from the South Oval. One comment said that the stadium rocked from the explosion, despite it later being found that such would have been impossible from the low power of the bomb.

With all of the differing opinions about whether the blast could even be heard, it is difficult to unravel the truth of the matter. Rumors began to swirl about a terrorist who had attempted to sneak into the stadium and a brave security guard who had stopped him. People began to wonder how many thousands might have been killed if he had managed to get past.

Bus driver Donald Laughlin actually saw the explosion. While he was sitting with his bus on the South Oval, waiting to pick up passengers when the game ended, he noticed a young man on a bench next to the GL Cross Microbiology building. He was leaning over a backpack that sat in his lap. In an instant, the backpack flashed, and all the driver could see was "a cloud of gray smoke as well as a human arm" detached from what remained of the young man.

Police quickly set up a perimeter, shuffling perplexed fans to exit through the east side of the stadium, away from the South Oval. Dogs trained to sniff out explosives searched every corner of the area for any other potential threat. A second explosion occurred, sending some into panic. However, as the press and administration at the university tried to explain, it was only a precaution. A suspicious package was found, taken to the detonation trailer and blown up by police. It was found not to contain any explosives, and the echoing second bang was only the police detonation equipment.

At the blast site, police were able to learn the identity of the young man who had died in the explosion from the wallet still in his back pocket. He was Joel Henry Hinrichs III, a junior at the school, only twenty-one years old and a National Merit Scholar. Norman bomb squad police analyzed the remains of the explosive and deemed it amateur at best. One member said that the victim was probably messing around with something he shouldn't have and that it was only a matter of time before he hurt himself.

Despite the isolation of the incident, or perhaps because of it, rumors began to fly around the town. Supposed eyewitnesses claimed that the terrorist had attempted to enter Gate 6 and was stopped by a guard suspicious about his backpack. The young man refused and "sprinted off" toward the South Oval. People called for an award to the security guard who had kept a terrorist from killing so many.

As the university looked into the story, however, it was shown that Joel, who preferred to be called "Joe," had not been sold a ticket. As a student, he would have used his ID to purchase entry into the stadium, but his name had never been entered into the ticket roster. He would not have gotten past the ticketing gate, let alone to where a security guard would ask to search his bag. Further, if the guard had asked to see the bag and the young man refused and ran away, why had the guard not radioed in the suspicious activity? After careful review of the security camera footage from the stadium, which has recordings of all entrances into the stadium, it was found that Joe had not attempted to enter the stadium at all.

While the Norman police concluded their report, the word of "terrorism" caused the Federal Bureau of Investigation to descend on the town and reevaluate the investigation. It was found that, earlier in the week, Joe had gone to Ellison Feed & Seed on Porter Avenue and inquired about ammonia nitrate. Oklahomans are quite familiar with the chemical, used as an industrial fertilizer as well as the 1995 bombing of the Murrah Building in Oklahoma City.

General Manager Dustin Ellison asked what Joe was planning for the ammonia nitrate and how much he needed. Joe, a novice to large explosives and with no experience in farming, had no real answers. Finally, Ellison told him that they did not carry any and offered different supplies, asking whether Joe was planning to "green up the yard." Joe replied, "Something like that," excused himself and left.

An off-duty Norman police officer happened to be in the store and took down Joe's description and tag as he drove away. The officer filed a report, but it was still in review in the police department on Saturday when Joe met his end on the South Oval.

A new wave of rumors began when it was released that police had gone to Joe's nearby apartment and found further explosives. There were a number of ingredients for bomb-making, including chemicals and equipment such as slow cookers and detonators. Empty artillery shells that had been purchased from eBay lay scattered on his floor. While neighbors looked on and were questioned, police made several trips in and out of the apartment to clear all of the dangerous material out of Joe's room. People began to whisper about Joe as a member of some kind of organization bent on mass destruction.

Things got worse when the public discovered that Joe's roommate was from Pakistan and a Muslim. Immediately upon word of the explosion on campus, the Islamic community in Oklahoma braced itself for an onslaught of suspicion, prejudice and outright verbal attack. An editorial appeared in the paper describing Joe as perfect material for a terrorist organization and noting that he "lived in proximity to 'international' students," as well as Norman's mosque. Other editorials noted that, had Joe intended to harm anyone other than himself, he would not have needed to get into the stadium itself. On game days, the whole campus is packed with crowds in the thousands. He had to find an isolated spot purposely, which he did on the bench set away from the sidewalk.

Nonetheless, Joe's Pakistani roommate, as well as two other Muslim students, were placed under arrest and taken for questioning. After several hours, it became clear that they had no knowledge of any terrorist activities or really even of Joe's personal activities. Joe's roommate admitted that he did not socialize with him. Fellow members of the Muslim Student Association described the roommate as a "really, really nice guy," and investigations proved that he had no connections with terrorist groups foreign or at home. Not even associating with his roommate, Joe was very much a loner, except for his classes and his membership in the Triangle fraternity.

Without a lead on any organization tied to the Middle East, the FBI began investigating Triangle. Agents lined up students and took names, even setting up a station for questioning in the house. Triangles were lambasted for hours, the FBI working to ensure that no one changed a story or gave up a detail that could point to homegrown terrorism. Memories of the mathematician Unabomber were still fresh in the minds of everyone, and the house of computer scientists and engineers suddenly seemed very suspicious.

Throughout the investigation, the Triangles proved themselves innocent. They knew Joe as one of their brothers, a quiet, awkward and angry member of the frat, but with no clear distinction of terrorist activity. The Triangles were well aware of Joe's fascination with explosives, and some had even gone with him on expeditions out in unpopulated areas of Oklahoma, where they could safely set off homemade devices for the same thrill felt by patriots every Fourth of July. When asked about their knowledge of homemade explosives, it was noted that anyone with access to the Internet has access to the infamous *Anarchist's Cookbook*.

Finally, after multiple turns under rigorous examination, one exhausted Triangle raised his hand to the FBI agents, waved it gently and told them, "These are not the droids you're looking for." Quoting *Star Wars* made it clear that the fraternity had passed the point of cracking, if there had been any secrets to crack, and the FBI closed its investigation in Norman.

Police and reporters alike also interviewed Joe's father, Joel Hindrichs Jr., a programmer living in the family home in Colorado Springs. His father said that there was no way to sum up his son. The young man had been a genius student but had also often suffered from bouts with depression. He described him as "very bright and very alone," frustrated and angry much of the time and having trouble fitting into social situations. In his second semester at the university, he began struggling and missing classes but was attending counseling sessions.

When asked about his fascination with explosives, the father replied that most boys seem drawn to their excitement and power. Joe was no exception. He said that when Joe had been thirteen or fourteen years old, he had built a bomb out of match heads, filling up an old CO_2 canister and watching it blow up. He brought the wreckage of the blast to his father with a "look of awe in his eyes."

Still, his father doubted that he meant anyone any harm. A high school coach confirmed that Joe was "a good kid" but got carried away with his fascination of explosives and ammunition. As to the rumor that Joe might have joined an extremist organization, his father replied that Joe was skeptical of ideology. The same problems relating to others that caused his depression prevented him from being a candidate in any kind of closely tied and secretive institution. Instead, Joe was among the Triangles, who, according to their minutes, spent meetings discussing how to carve a club out of a tree branch and making road trips to Las Vegas.

In the fall of 2005, Joe's life took a downward turn. His grades fell, and he began having trouble sleeping. Despite outward signs of planning for the future, such as studying and discussing a new car with his father, Joe became suicidal. He was unable to vent frustrations and so decided to end it in the most appropriate way he knew: a bomb.

No one knows why Joe came to campus that game day. Many suppose it was to take as many people with him as he could, but this is clearly not the case. As university president David Boren assured the press, it was an isolated case of suicide, a tragedy, not a threat to the safety of the school. During investigations into his apartment, his laptop was found with a word processor still open to a document in which he appeared to be taking notes for himself. A single line of text was on the screen, aligned so that it served almost as a suicide note. "F___ all this. None of you are worth living with."

The impact caused by Joe's suicide went beyond the physical damage of a replaced bench, a tree that had to be carefully pruned of its lost branches and a blood-spattered bus. According to a couple who served as his roommate's host parents during the Pakistani student's first year in America, despite changing his name and moving to a different city, no one will hire him as background checks show a police interrogation in his history. Joe's brother, too, served jail time after extensive questioning by the FBI caused him to make an angry and ill-advised blanket threat toward the Bureau. While the statement was made out of aggravation, it was taken very seriously, and the Hinrichs family felt yet more tragedy.

Memory of the explosion also lives on at the isolated bench tucked next to the microbiology building. Students usually avoid the bench. It is out of the way, as it is set back from the sidewalk, but the spot looks lovely with its regrown trees and background of the brick façade on Cross. Those who know what happened there have mostly graduated and gone on, but there still remains an air of unhappiness around the bench.

An uneasy feeling wells up in people who sit on the bench long. Rather than typical ghostly impressions, with sensations of being watched or detecting a presence, the feeling is strictly an emotional one. Moods become depressed, and people become agitated. Despite the beautiful view of the sprawling South Oval, the world seems to come crushing down on them.

Paranormal investigators have attempted to take EVPs at the site to see if the spirit of Joe lingers around the area where he perished, but no recorded voices have yet been heard. Perhaps he is as unable to communicate vocally from the beyond even as he was in life. However, there is still the impression of his somber mood. It seems like a final chance to share at last the frustration and depression of someone who needed so badly to relate to his fellow human beings.

Neighbors who were questioned by police searching Joe's apartment confessed to knowing almost nothing about him. The people who lived in the next-door apartment, their bedroom buffering against his—their lives literally only inches apart—admitted, "We have no idea what's on that side of the wall."

If we took greater interest in those around us, perhaps those like Joe who struggle day to day might still be among us in more than solemn memories and dark impressions.

Part III
Haunts of Campus Corner and Beyond

As soon as Norman laid its claim to host the territorial university, a business community grew up around the potential campus. Students came from all over the new Oklahoma and brought with them needs for food, housing and entertainment beyond textbooks and the classroom. The administration did not allow students to have cars, so these needs had to be met within walking distance. Thus, Campus Corner was born.

As the university grew, so did Campus Corner and the rest of the area of town around the campus. Students brought in demand for housing just as they do today. Boardinghouses lined the streets of Norman, giving students a place to rest their heads and fill their bellies. Many of the early students were single males who were housed in the local Young Men's Christian Association, where rooms were cheap if inelegant. Enterprising Normanites built up houses for students to rent. Faculty such as Dean Holmberg and President Boyd made their homes there.

Beyond housing, Campus Corner became filled with laundromats, like the original Clark's Cleaners; clothing stores, such as McCall's in 1935, which eventually became the famous Harold's fine clothing; shops, including one of Oklahoma's first TG&Y's; and anything else the students could possibly need and be willing to pay for. Restaurants became common in the area as cafeterias on campus and in Greek houses did not serve on the weekends. Even during the week, eateries were popular places to go for a meal away from the repetitious meals of campus. Restaurants, and especially bars, offered other escapes through beer, cigarettes and music. Establishments such as Fred Swisher's Varsity Shop at 225 West Boyd gave a stage to the popular Pinky Tomlan Band, which would bring to the world songs such as "Tiptoe Through the Tulips." The iconic Boomer Theater sprang up in 1947 as a movie house and later became a concert venue where many famous area musicians played in the '70s and '80s.

As Campus Corner grew up, it also became a place for students to celebrate away from the watchful eyes of university administration. What might make a dean of students frown on campus was perfectly allowed just across the street. In preparation for home games, students lit bonfires at street corners and raced up and down with horns and colored flags. Most of the restaurants, shops and especially bars kept dance parlors on their second floors. One business, known as the Organ Grinder, specialized in dancing, but certainly not the kind that would be spoken about in mixed company.

Because of the cultural ties beyond simple economics of providing services to students, Campus Corner and the university have created a symbiotic relationship where one cannot change without the other changing in kind. When the YMCA burned in 1922, the balance of life in

Campus Corner, famous for its eateries and shops.

Campus Corner was so thrown off that the student body saw the need for a Union building on campus. The infamous Organ Grinder was for a time owned by the Engineers Club. To this day, the connection continues to grow deeper as the OU IT store opened on the north side of Boyd Street along with lecture space.

Campus Corner carries a fair number of hidden corners where life carries on after death. Old boardinghouses turned into trinket shops still creak with the spirits of veterans returning from World War II. A man greeted his brother's landlord in the restaurant he leased and then realized that the old landlord had passed away two weeks before. All through the twisting blocks of shops and the neighborhoods beyond, college spirit never ends.

POLITE GHOSTS

Whitehand Hall

A huge building looking like a brick cathedral stands at the top of the North Oval. Its bell tower soars above everything nearby, even dwarfing some of the nearby churches. While landscaping makes the ground level inviting, the small doors set into wide brick walls gives any visitor a sense of unease. Strange stone figures and Latin phrases rest over many of the doors. Students rarely go to Whitehand, and few are surprised to hear that it is haunted.

Whitehand was built by Scottish Rite Freemasons in 1921, explaining the cryptic symbols that decorate the building. Masons out of Chickasha were given a $300,000 grant from the Masonic Charity Foundation of Oklahoma to erect a dormitory for participants in the newly founded DeMolay International. Named after Jacques de Molay, the final grand master of the Knights Templar, the organization aimed to improve young men and foster leadership. The offer of a free place to live while studying at the university greatly encouraged membership.

Freemasonry had become very popular as fraternities grew up in the newly founded Oklahoma, where men were eager to be seen as progressive. The fraternity was officially founded to improve leadership and morality among its members. A bonus came, however, as leaders sought to be Masons, making it an excellent opportunity to network for an elevated status in society and business.

Above: Whitehand Hall at night.

Below: A Masonic emblem still hanging over Whitehand's door.

The dormitory was given the name Albert Pike Hall after the famed Confederate general and longtime sovereign grand commander of the Southern Scottish Rite Freemasons. Pike, following an adventurous life as an explorer and newspaperman, left the war early after unfounded accusations of war crimes and treason prompted his disappearance, eventual arrest and resignation. The rest of his career was dedicated to fraternal orders, primarily the Masons, and he is the only Confederate general with a statue in Washington, D.C.

The hall housed young Masons for twenty years, but the Great Depression caused the organization to go into decline, as members could no longer afford dues and government programs took over the work that charity had done before. It was sold to the university in 1946 and renamed Whitehand Hall after Captain Robert Whitehand. He had served the university's drama department, writing many of the plays performed on campus. In 1942, he left teaching to serve in World War II in the U.S. Army Air Corps, where he hoped he would find great inspiration for future works. However, he perished while fighting over France in 1945, and the popular professor was mourned by his fellow faculty, students and staff.

When World War II ended, a flood of returning veterans suddenly had the opportunity to attend college through the G.I. Bill. OU became inundated with incoming students and sought any student housing available. For married students, blocks of prefabricated homes were set up south of campus nicknamed "Sooner City." For unmarried male veterans, homes and halls were purchased on Campus Corner, including Albert Pike. Whitehand was soon filled again with boisterous male students, who informally referred to the dorm as the "Oklahoma Hotel."

The housing crisis ended, and Whitehand was converted to offices, but it seems to continue to serve as home to a number of spirits seeking a place to stay while wandering the earth. Whispers and even louder voices without bodies trickle through the halls. In addition, footsteps and unexplainable noises ring in the night and even during daytime. Most often, they are heard by employees working late at their desks.

The whispers are so common that workers have simply become used to them. No one pays them too much heed, and a few even enjoy the sounds, describing them as "a symphony of voices." If the voices become too distracting, people simply go home. A few have attempted to tell the voices to hush, with varying degrees of success. Some of the spirits seem well meaning, while a few are genuinely disruptive.

In 2007, Carol, mother of one of the employees, invited the Contact Research Investigation Specialist (CRIS) team to spend a night in Whitehand Hall. CRIS was founded by Lisa Ghariani to focus on capturing EVPs, auditory contacts with spiritual beings. Using sensitive sound equipment, CRIS records everything throughout the night and then spends weeks carefully listening to the playback for voices that belong to no mortal present.

Throughout the night, Ghariani and her team explored the building. An automatic door was believed to be haunted as it would open and close itself, but their electrical expert determined that there was a short in the wiring and fixed it. There were no physical or visual manifestations. There was a great deal of EVP captured, however, from what Ghariani called "the most polite ghost we've ever met."

CRIS classifies its EVPs into three categories: A) a readily apparent and clear voice; B) a garbled but distinguishable voice; and C) a voice difficult to make out but otherwise unexplainable. Much of the evening's communications from the spirit realm were B-rated, focusing around the first floor and basement. Ghariani led sessions in which questions were posed and answers, while not heard by the human ear, could later be deciphered from the quiet background. Taking inspiration from the decades of research by Sara Estep, Ghariani begins her sessions by requesting a "monitor" from the other side to help proctor and connect the worlds. Doing so increased her collection of EVPs tenfold with much better quality.

Their most talkative voice introduced itself. "My name is Edwards." He even repeated himself and added, "I told you." Soon thereafter, the voice replied to Ghariani's questions with, "I'm standing right here" and "Pleased to meet you."

The voice returned for a third time, saying, "Tell Carol there is something here." Not only is the spirit polite enough to introduce himself, but he also shows coherency with the mortal realm and even concern. Rather than leaving Carol wondering, he was happy to tell her that there is nothing to be concerned about.

Despite research, there has not been a particular "Mr. Edwards" noted in the history of Whitehand Hall. However, with so many men having lived in the dormitory through its years, it is possible that one Mr. Edwards may have returned to the place he cherished as a college home.

In addition to Edwards, another, softer voice may be heard, which Ghariani believes is a monitor. Something whispered, perhaps directed at Edwards, "No time to tell them you're guilty."

Right: The halls of Whitehand have been gutted and remodeled.

Below: Whitehand Hall, once a dormitory for young Masons.

If the voice is, in fact, a proctor from the spirit world, this widens the mystery of Mr. Edwards or one of the other spirits said to whisper in the night. Rather than being a wandering spirit, it seems that he has some sort of connection with Whitehand (or perhaps Albert Pike) Hall. Some unfinished business or unconfessed crime seems to be keeping him there. As polite as he is, it is difficult to imagine him performing some unforgivable sin, but there has always been a purposeful air of mystery around Freemasonry, of which he may have been a part.

A Haunted Bakery

Café Plaid

One of the most famous restaurants on Campus Corner is the privately owned and operated Café Plaid. It prides itself on its sustainable business practices and provides only "100% Fair Trade and 100% Certified Organic Coffee." Often viewed as a "hippie joint," the restaurant is patronized by more liberal Normanites as well as those who simply enjoy the taste and atmosphere. Jokes have it that Café Plaid exists because of the drama department on campus across the street, along with the other members of Fine Arts, who also claim ownership of the foodie hotspot.

Café Plaid has two wide rooms filled with any kind of seating a restaurant patron could desire: tables both round and square, booths and raised tables and bars with stools. The western wall is packed with its coffee bar, featuring drinks caffeinated or not, with every kind of flavor at any range of temperature. In the back, hungry students and Normanites alike line up for specialty sandwiches and salads. The café carries a smooth ambience with old wooden floors, art from local artists lining the walls and posters of Norman events plastered on the windows.

While busy at meal times, the café slows down in the between hours to a casual pace. The atmosphere is laidback, and workers are usually as cheerful and relaxed as the patrons. Students frequenting the arts area of campus often retire to Café Plaid to decompress from studying or to do their studying there with easy access to non-Starbucks coffee. The food draws them in as well, particularly the freshly baked focaccia bread and pastries made in a bakery that is rumored to be haunted by a rowdy poltergeist.

Café Plaid, known for its sandwiches freshly made in the restaurant's bakery.

Spilling salt seems to upset the spirit that haunts the bakery. Soon after a hapless baker or helper in the small kitchen bumps the salt canister over, letting a few white grains tumble to the floor, strange activity often begins to happen. It does not seem to do it with every chef, but there are those whom the spirit seems to have targeted, as if telling them they should know better.

Without anyone touching them or even vibrations from across the table or shelf, things begin to fall over. An invisible hand seems to smack them, knocking over everything from flour bowls to timers on stands to cups full of utensils. Different people in the bakery have different strategies for dealing with the sudden poltergeist. Some apologize, others rush to clean up the salt in the hopes the spirit might not notice and some simply leave the bakery until the spirit's tantrum is done.

The ghostly presence is most felt by Café Plaid's baker, Sara Hughes. She arrives "early, early" every morning, which is typically when activity seems at its most boisterous. On one occasion, the noisy ghost seemed to focus on a pan guard kept inside its appropriate pan underneath the metal worktable in the middle of the room. It is a standard steel square, the type tucked into a fitting pan to allow bread to rise tall and then be easily removed from the pan below after baking. That morning, as Sara was stepping out of the bakery to do something else, she heard a clatter.

She looked back into the bakery to find a pan guard on the floor. Everything else on the stack of metal bake ware was untouched. Since the pan guard was already fit into the pan, something must have lifted it to toss it out. Otherwise, the pan would have fallen, too. Sara decided not to think much of it and supposed that the pan guard had been placed inappropriately. Sara put it back and then went about her work.

A few minutes later, the familiar clatter rang again. Again, the pan was still in its untouched position on the rack beneath the table. Again, next to the table on the floor, was the pan guard. Something had lifted it and tossed it aside for reasons that Sara could not fathom. This time, she left the pan guard where it was and let the ghost have its way.

Most often, the ghost seems to tinker with the timers used for baking. A skeptic might point out that timers could have flaws in their electronics, but the issues are sporadic and random enough to discount simple mechanical problems. On a number of occasions, multiple timers bug out simultaneously.

The ghost enjoys the sound or at least the reactions from people jumping to a beep that no one had set. It does not seem to tamper with the time, spoiling bread by not having the timer go off early or by letting the timer go too long and burning the bread. Instead, it simply pulls a prank now and again, such as the case with the large main timer in the bakery. One morning, the timer suddenly jumped to life with a loud, unending shriek. Sara hit buttons to stop it, but the beep continued until she pulled the batteries out. When she put them in again, the timer worked perfectly well. Soon after, one of the timers over the cooktop in the main kitchen went off, even though Sara was the only one there.

After several such instances, Sara became fed up with the ghost's actions seemingly pulling pranks behind her back. One morning she finally announced, "If there's someone here, show yourself!" Nothing happened in reply. Sara shrugged at herself and left the bakery. When she returned, the front right burner on the industrial stove had turned itself on. A one-foot-tall flame burst up from the burner with enough force to blow the grating, weighing about three pounds, completely off. She decided that she had her sign and quickly turned the stove off.

Sara is not the only employee to have witnessed paranormal phenomena. Several of the staff at Café Plaid have spotted a white apparition walking

The stovetop in the Café Plaid bakery said to have exploded in a ghostly sign.

in the lobby area among the tables. It does not seem to carry any specific details, just the outline of a white body with head, arms and sometimes legs. Sometimes it stands still, as if watching the employee in return or simply staring into space. Other times it has been seen moving, gliding silently among the tables before inevitably disappearing.

The most whispered-about event happened one night when a staff member named Taylor and another Café Plaid worker were closing up for the evening. They had locked up, cleared the tables and made sure that the kitchens were clean. Finally turning out the overhead lights, they sat in the far corner of the restaurant with only a lamp and popped open a couple of "shift beers" to celebrate the end of another workday.

Suddenly, a horrific noise began to ring from the bakery. They jumped up to inspect and found the speakers blaring. Borrowed from an old computer set, the speakers are used to pipe in music and entertain staff while they bake. Rather than being connected to a radio, the speakers are usually hooked up to an mp3 player so that workers can enjoy custom playlists. On this night, the wire was dangling bare, with no mp3 player in sight. The speakers had been cranked to full volume and played out crackling white noise.

Taylor and his co-worker turned off the speakers and wondered what it was all about. They checked for anyone else in the back, but the doors had been locked from the inside. They were alone. Feeling somewhat nervous, they decided to relax and finish their beers.

When they returned to the lobby, all of the overhead lights had turned themselves back on. These lights all tie to a control box behind the coffee counter with mechanical sliding switches, meaning it could not have been ambient shifts in the air causing any kind of motion detector to go off. They checked the box, and sure enough, the switches had all been physically moved back into the "on" position.

They decided that relaxation was impossible at this point. Taylor and his co-worker turned the lights back off and quickly headed out the back door, leaving their shift beers behind.

No one is quite certain where the Café Plaid ghost would have come from. Although the building has been there for decades, there are no stories of mysterious deaths. Sara the baker was at first afraid that she had brought it with her, as her old job had its share of strange activity, but co-workers assured her that the haunt was nothing new when she arrived. Whatever its reasons, the spirit seems to have no interest in leaving or, as Taylor and his workmate could attest, even letting the place close for the night.

Casa Blanca

103 West Boyd

The white building at the corner of Jenkins and Boyd has gone through decades as a lone structure while the world changed around it. As shops sprang up around it and the engineering quad expanded, what was once a prized sorority house became a dilapidated mess resting in the shadows of the towering Sarkey Energy Center. Through years of hard work, the "testy old broad" was turned back "into a beautiful, well-mannered lady" that even earned it a spot on National Register of Historic Places.

"Casa Blanca," as Normanites know it, began in 1925 as the new house for the Alpha Chi Omega sorority. It was built with fashionable Spanish Mission Revival architecture and became one of the classiest houses on campus. The Psi chapter of the Alpha Chi Omega sorority began in 1916 as an organization for female students associated with music. Mrs. Frederik Holmberg, wife of the dedicated Fine Arts dean, was instrumental in its founding and served as hostess leading the girls. Through her guidance, the sorority expanded beyond its first house, then its second and at last built the eleven-bedroom house at Boyd and Jenkins.

As with any sorority, the popular Alpha Chi Omegas had their share of secrets. To maintain a firm sense of prim and proper modesty, the doors to the house were locked at 10:30 p.m. Any girl out after such an hour was bound to be up to undignified acts and, of course, would have no place in the sorority. However, at the back of the house leading up to the second

Once a sorority house and home for boarders, Casa Blanca is now an office building.

floor, a strong trellis was built. The trellis allowed vines to creep up, as well as a few girls sneaking in after curfew.

Other activities went on in the house that came to light as former residents came to tour the renovation and reminisce. A former houseboy, a kind of servant taken on by the house as someone to do heavy chores, recalled siphoning off the syrup from canned peaches and fermenting it into wine. The first floor, where the housemother's room was, had hardwood floors and easily mobile furniture that could turn the entire level into a dance hall with little notice.

The Alpha Chi Omegas eventually outgrew the house and moved to their new, larger house on College. The sorority house became a boardinghouse. It was repainted white and given a catchy nickname, "Casa Blanca." Soon, however, the house grew notorious as the "cheapest place to live" in Norman. The tenants attracted were of poorer and poorer quality, and the house fell into miserable disrepair. Finally, the business was closed. Still, the house lived on, hosting a number of illegal squatters and vagrants. Rumors spread about drugs and homicides inside the once-fashionable house.

Top: The lobby of Casa Blanca before the renovation. *Keith F. Walker Oil & Gas Company, LLC.*

Bottom: Pre-renovation hallway in Casa Blanca. *Keith F. Walker Oil & Gas Company, LLC.*

In 1988, Norman entrepreneur Jaci Williams bought the house when it came up at auction by the Federal Deposit Insurance Corporation after default. A $500,000 renovation later, the old sorority was turned into an office complex. Despite fresh stucco returning the house to its sandy peach color, the name Casa Blanca stuck.

One of the early tenants in the reinvigorated building was the campus recruiter for the United States Marine Corps. Strange activity began to occur soon after settling into the new office. Lights blinked on and off, more than flickering due to a faulty wire. At seemingly random intervals, the office scanner, connected to a computer, would start itself up, scanning a blank image from the top of the lid. Most peculiar of all was the phone system. All at once, the three lines would suddenly make loud simultaneous rings. Then they would go dead again.

The matters were investigated by the building manager, but no electrical problems could be found. Anyone brought in to search out a short or even a crossed wire saw that nothing was out of the ordinary. Most perplexing of all was that all three of the issues were on separate systems. The lights were tied to an electrical grid, the scanner had to be operated by its computer (which would have blinked off in the case of an electrical failure) and the phone lines have their own wires. Whatever was making the office equipment go berserk was doing so beyond the mechanical level.

A secretary for the recruiter blamed spirits from the sorority. She said that the male recruits would go down to the basement to change. While the basement is as unnerving as any, no one felt any particular threat. However, if she were to call up the young men too quickly, the electrical problems seemed to flare up almost instantly. She decided that the sorority gals had been enjoying peeping on the soldiers and were frustrated when their show ended all too early.

Casa Blanca is now occupied by the Keith F. Walker Oil & Gas Company. It was heavily modernized to include an updated Internet system, complete with a server room refitted from the old kitchen. While on the cutting edge of information technology features, it also fits well within the antique sense that gives the house its place on the National Register.

Employees at the Walkèr Company have had their own bewildering events. Rather than electrical, the paranormal activity takes place as sounds coming from different levels of the house.

Casa Blanca lobby post-renovation.

Alpha Chi Omega Sorority House. *Keith F. Walker Oil & Gas Company, LLC.*

In one instance, two workers had arrived early in the morning. They were on the first floor preparing to get some coffee to start their days when they heard footsteps walking down the hall above them. It was no mere groan as the building settled; the sounds made clear and distinct footsteps against the wooden floor. The two looked at each other and asked if either one had let someone else into the building, but neither had. The male employee ran upstairs to see if someone had broken into the house. Despite his search, there was no one on the second floor.

Another employee heard sounds coming from below. As she worked at her desk, through the vent to the basement, she heard a giggle, like the sound of a child's laughter. The laugh went on for some time, clearly a young person having a laughing fit. She got up, wondering how a kid had gotten into the basement. After a careful search there, the strange sounds again proved to have no body attached.

It is possible she mistook the child's laugh for a piece of equipment, such as the furnace, turning on, but she had sat at the same desk for months and would have become familiar with all of the various sounds emanating from below. Others wonder whether it was actually a child—perhaps it was more like the girlish giggle of a sorority member, having come back to dwell in the house she once considered home.

Connections

763 DeBarr Avenue and 707 West Boyd Street

The issue of mental health has always been a difficult one in Oklahoma. While progressive ideals have taken stage to build up excellent care and facilities, the cost of upkeep prove too much for many state legislators. Constantly facing issues of stretched resources and changing strategies in treatment, Norman's Griffin Memorial Hospital (once Central State Mental Hospital) began programs in the 1970s to reintegrate patients back into society as soon as possible and lessen the burden on the state.

Patients with a degree of independence are let off the main campus that also houses the Oklahoma Community Mental Health Center. While some patients still have rooms on the grounds and return to them, others take up residence in halfway houses. The facilities provide a base in communal living, giving patients stability and working to expose them to the world outside in the hopes that they might soon live on their own. In other instances, lack of funding prompts patients who might do better in more structured environments to leave before they are ready. They often rent rooms near Campus Corner, where living space is cheap and within easy walking distance of shops, the same reasons college students rent them.

One such house stands just north of campus on DeBarr Avenue. It is a spacious building with a wide porch, large communal rooms on the first floor and stairs leading up to the bedrooms on the second. The outside is painted a charming light blue. However, since being shut down years ago, it has fallen into disrepair. The windows are boarded up, the doors have been posted with "No Trespassing" signs and various boards have come loose.

The building was once owned by Dr. Harry and Thekla Mendros as part of the Connections program that rented rooms to mentally ill former patients who previously lived on the hospital grounds. Dr. Mendros was a psychiatrist who saw need to house patients, although he did not rent to his own patients on ethical grounds. The program had already fallen under a great deal of suspicion in 1995 when a patient died under mysterious circumstances.

On March 12, 1995, forty-eight-year-old Richard Shepherd died of seizures in another Connections building, Newman Hall at 707 West Boyd. The large gray building had been built in 1926 as a dormitory for Catholic female students attending the university by the parish of St. Thomas More. As housing became more standardized on campus, the parish sold

The old Connections House on DeBarr Avenue.

the building to become a boardinghouse. It came under the ownership of Connections, who used it as housing for disabled patients.

Normanites still remember the old Newman Hall. One man recalled his work as a pizza deliveryman while in college and a delivery to the Connections center there. He said that when he entered the building, the secretary at the desk jumped in fright. She looked terrified and sleepless, as if nervous about every move. Another woman recalled visiting the center and watching four patients play cards without a deck. They went through the motions of shuffling, dealing and laying out their cards, all with empty hands.

Upon Shepherd's death, an investigation began as to why his system did not have the medication he needed. Cuts and bruises found over Shepherd's body were believed to have been made before his death, as if his final seizure had been one of a series over several days. Shepherd's daughter accused the center of withholding medication, as her father was hopeful to leave the center someday to be with his grandchildren and pursue his hobby of collecting rocks.

Newman Hall, once a Connections house, on Boyd Street.

Other patients began coming forward with reports of embezzlement. One noted that his bank account was missing more than $800; investigators began to uncover potentially thousands of dollars that had disappeared in the years before. Kim Moore, an assistant administrator there, suddenly disappeared after a meeting with police. She was later charged with forging checks and stealing rent checks from patients.

Charges in the death investigation were later dropped due to a lack of evidence. Although Connections itself was not found at fault, the bad press prompted state legislators to close off their funding for the next fiscal year. Newman Hall was soon closed down, but the house on DeBarr kept going until the next year.

On May 24, 1996, Cameron Lee Smith was seen walking naked through Campus Corner carrying a backpack. He dropped the backpack in a dumpster and then walked back to his room at the DeBarr house. A curious Normanite decided to check what the naked man had been trying to throw away. He dug into the dumpster, found the backpack and opened it to reveal a disembodied human head.

Smith had gotten into an argument with one of his housemates, Roydon Major, who lived less than thirty feet away from him. They quarreled over something about cigarettes, a fight Smith solved by using a sharp, pointed knife to stab Major over and over again. He decapitated Major, decided to strip off his own bloody clothes and then walked outside to dispose of him. When police arrived, they found Smith sitting in the bathtub cleaning up. His blood-soaked clothes were still sitting on his bedroom floor.

Smith was partially deaf and wore hearing aids in both ears. He was "unresponsive and appeared dazed," making police processing difficult and requiring the courtroom bailiff at his court appearance to repeat the judge's words standing directly in front of Smith and shouting. Still, Smith indicated that he understood the accusation of murder and that he wished to have a lawyer. He was later found incompetent to stand trial, but as there were no maximum-security beds available on the mental health campuses, he remained in jail.

Norman residents began to grow fearful over the idea of the mentally ill living among them. Mental health officials stated that such fears were unfair. Rob Lee, director of the Community Mental Health Center, rebutted attacks of former patients being dangers to the community with statistical evidence that "as a population, the mentally ill are less violent than the general population."

Yet the stigma remained. The mayor attempted to find a peaceful solution, but every rezoning request was suddenly viewed by very suspicious eyes. The Mendroses, meanwhile, became inundated by phone calls from nervous and angry Normanites, as well as curious members of the media. The house had been shut down since the murder for "remodeling," according to Mrs. Mendros. Still, it was besieged by media to the point that their son and acting landlord, George Mendros, threatened to call the police on any more reporters trespassing.

Eventually, the rumor storm blew over, but by that time, Connections was no more. Instead, the house was rented to students and locals without histories of mental illness. One group pooled its resources to rent the whole house and then "packed it with two dozen hippies." Bumper stickers and cheerful graffiti still decorate the outer walls of the house from its time as a commune.

While the new residents were there, they noted strange activity both inside and around the house. Footsteps were heard coming from the upper floor even when everyone was downstairs. Sometimes the steps would walk down the stairs, each one thumping and creaking in turn without any body there to make the sound. Other indescribable noises were heard. People were unsure whether they heard whispers or groans or outright voices. The more people asked about the sounds and tried to investigate, the more they seemed to hear. Gradually, the house began to give out dark vibes. The tenants decided to leave it and go their separate ways.

The house also once served as communal living.

Even stranger than the sounds were the visions of people hanging in the trees just outside the windows. Rumors among the residents stated that some of the previous housemates had committed suicide by hanging themselves. While unconfirmed, the story seemed verified by people glancing outside and believing they saw bodies swinging in the breeze. Some had ropes attached to them, and others simply floated there impossibly among the branches.

The house is now unoccupied and under new ownership of local restaurateurs. They began remodeling it in the hopes of renting out the house to new residents, but their work was interrupted. While the house seemingly needed minor repairs and painting, something about it seemed to reject change. The new owners would fix one thing, and another would suddenly break. Rebuilding became too much for them, and they finally decided to let it sit empty until something was resolved about the bad energy of the house.

Neighbors are wary of the house not only as a potential hangout for vagrants but also from its suspicious nature. Workers at the nearby Pad Thai restaurant are free to park their cars in the lot behind the wall next to the house, but few are willing to do it. One server there said that she did park there before, but as she came out of the restaurant, she felt as if something in the house were watching her. While she confessed that she was probably only scaring herself, the sensation of being spied on was so intense that she now always parks up the street, keeping trees between her and the house.

Trees line the edges of the old house.

Newman Hall also carries an odd feeling about it. The university purchased the property and uses it for storage for props and costumes from the drama department. Passersby avoid looking at the building, which gave a similar sensation of unseen eyes watching from the dark windows. Improvements in landscaping and white boards being posted over the windows have helped a bit.

Inside, the strange feelings continue to flow strongly. Students and staff rarely go into the building, and only when school business demands it. Among the storage rooms, people feel constantly as if they are being watched and followed. Items being stored are meticulously placed, but when people come to fetch them, they are notoriously moved or disassembled. Some frequenters of the storage rooms say that they have felt hands touching them, stroking shoulders, arms and hair.

THE PIONEER WOMAN

Brandt Park

Also known as the "Duck Pond," Brandt Park has undergone a number of changes during its existence as a public space. It is among the earliest parts of land to be known as "Norman." In the 1870s, government surveyors followed the cattle drives, attempting to firmly map out the unknown lands in the western part of Indian Territory. The Arbuckle Trail led up through Norman and eventually fed into the famed Chisholm Trail to the west, winding its way to the cattle yards of Dodge City, Kansas. A team under twenty-three-year-old Abner Norman followed the trail, making camp on the hill where Classen and Lindsey Streets meet today.

According to town legend, as a joke the men painted a sign celebrating their young leader and dubbing their encampment "Norman's Camp." They attached it to an elm tree, which would have grown close to the creek bed where it still runs today. In years to come, the railroad came through the same spot, and engineers made use of the name. By the time of the land run, "Norman" had stuck.

In the early days of the twentieth century, Brandt Park was an undeveloped lot east of the campus grounds that made up the gap between the school and the railroad tracks running down from Oklahoma City toward Dallas. It was initially a small floodplain for the creek that eventually feeds into the Canadian River south of town. Wild animals lived in the trees that lined the water, some of the only tall vegetation in the entire town before OU President Boyd began his project of planting tens of thousands of trees in town at personal expense.

The influx of vegetation helped save much of Norman from the ravages of the Dust Bowl in Oklahoma. When the Great Depression settled on the

United States and the world, Oklahoma, which had just seen one of the worst natural disasters ever to hit the nation, became a prime candidate for projects to rebuild. The Works Progress Administration stepped in to fund projects planned by state and local governing bodies. Oklahoma, which already had welfare programs in place as relief for the Dust Bowl and its own collapsed economy, gained a generous share of national funding. WPA money built schools, bridges, sidewalks, public buildings and the Duck Pond.

The project was the brainchild of famed Oklahoma football coach Bennie Owen. Retired since 1926, he had a vision for the undeveloped land to become a nine-hole golf course. His drive brought support from the town, which gained federal money to turn Owen's dream into a reality. The land was leveled and planted with smoother grass. A dam was built alongside the road to control water levels, backing up enough water to form a small lake as a water hazard. Stone fences and bridges were set up to give the golf course an Old World feel right in what was fast becoming the heart of Norman.

The golf course was dubbed Brandt Park in honor of the university's president, but locals quickly came to know it as the "Duck Pond." Every Easter, cute ducklings were given as presents to children as part of the spring celebration. In the weeks after, the ducklings would grow up into unmanageable older ducks that were loud, required a great deal of cleanup and often turned mean. To alleviate the family, parents would take their ducks down to the golf course lake and let them go. The activity became a yearly custom, and soon the Duck Pond began a stable local population of former Easter ducks.

As the years went on, the duck issue grew out of hand as the flock began taking over and chasing away potential golfers. City officials began a new tradition of rounding up excess ducks and donating them every Thanksgiving and Christmas to dinners at the Norman Municipal Hospital. Eventually, the practice was deemed barbaric, and instead the duck population was thinned every two years by transplanting the excess fowl to Lake Thunderbird to the east. A new ecological balance was struck, and the Duck Pond became a facet of campus.

Over time, silt began to build up in the Duck Pond as the ducks and other wildlife gradually undid what Owen had dreamed. A student initiative began in the 1960s and '70s to clean out the pond, but it became doomed when the cost in money and man-hours of the project was calculated. Gradually, the Duck Pond and the surrounding park turned into "a swamp." Where children had once happily fed the ducks, they were now chased by eager rats seeking to grab the bread out of their hands. A fetid smell wafted

The Duck Pond in Brandt Park.

up from the silty pond and increasing wetlands around. The duck-laden young families and eager golfers who once patronized the park avoided it. It became a haunt where the homeless were known to sleep. Students only visited when they wished to be alone for activities that could not be witnessed going into their bedrooms.

In 1983, staff from the OU Police Department began a fund under the title "Friends of the Duck Pond." Seeing the filth of the pond too often on their rounds as they were called to break up disturbances, the police decided to solve the problem by returning the Duck Pond to its former days of glory. Over the next thirty months, some seven thousand hours of volunteer time and more than $250,000 were spent revitalizing the park and turning it into a community asset. For twenty years, the Norman Medieval Fair set up camp every April in the park, along with a fundraising booth to continue park improvements. New trees and facilities have gone up with well-managed landscaping. Most recently, a well-lit serpentine walk popular with joggers was constructed to line the park. With patrons returning to the park, there have also been increased sightings of the famed Pioneer Woman ghost.

She is described as wearing a dress and bonnet that would have been customary fashion in the late nineteenth century. The dress is faded, often described as a soft blue, and she is often looking away from the person who sees her. On other occasions, people picnicking glance up to see her watching them. They sometimes call to her or get up to see what she wants, prompting her to vanish.

Rumors about what brought the woman to haunt the park are varied. Some state that she is a girlfriend following after her cowboy lover. She fell behind, succumbed due to exposure to what was then wilderness and now still roams the park, searching for her lost beloved.

Other rumors say that she is one of the original pioneers in the Unassigned Lands. Whether through violent means or natural causes, her life was cut short. Still, she refuses to give up the land, a Sooner spirit working for progress even from beyond the grave.

MEX

Owen Field

The University of Oklahoma has had a varied history of mascots. Even the team name has changed, as the original college teams were known as the "Rough Riders" after Colonel (and then President) Theodore Roosevelt's band of cavalry in the Spanish-American War. In 1908, the team name changed to the "Sooners," which first came from the pep club known as the "Sooner Rooters." The term had initially meant those who legally (or illegally) entered the Unassigned Lands earlier than the Land Run of 1889, and many used it as a slur for those with unfair advantages. As the years passed, the term was liberated and redefined during the Progressive movement to mean an individual with hardworking optimism and ambition.

Defining a Sooner was difficult enough, and finding a mascot to match was not an easy task. It would not be until 1980 that the Sooner Schooner, a covered wagon from the days of pioneers in the West, became the official mascot. The wagon, driven by the Roughneck male pep squad, began its course in 1964 and worked its way into authorized Sooner fandom. It is pulled by two ponies, Boomer and Sooner, who are cared for by the Roughnecks at a nearby farm. In 2005, the athletics program introduced twin mascots in horse costumes, bringing Boomer and Sooner to interact with crowds and participate in charity events. As beloved as Boomer and Sooner are today, the early days of OU had its own mascot that seemingly ruled the school: Mex the Dog.

In 1914, a young Oklahoman named Mott Keys from Hollis joined the U.S. Army's medical corps. He was stationed on the Mexican border, watching over the revolution there that had produced rebels such as Pancho Villa, who had stormed several towns in New Mexico and put them to the torch. Tensions were high, and Keys's company found relief when it discovered an abandoned litter of puppies while on patrol. Keys adopted one of the young Boston terriers and named him "Mex."

Mex came home with Keys to Hollis and then to the University of Oklahoma when Keys enrolled. Thanks to Keys's knowledge of field medicine, he joined the staff of the growing OU Athletic Department as a medic. Mex came along with him, at first being used as a deterrent to wandering dogs that might come onto the field, which at the time were literal fields borrowed for sports. Keys and Mex also joined the Kappa Sigma fraternity, where the brothers taught Mex to celebrate along with them whenever Oklahoma scored. At touchdowns, Mex would give "a joyous staccato bark." Mex also came along to baseball games, where each homerun was greeted with a "victory woof."

Mex became a staple at games. He was presented with a little red sweater with white stripes, as well as a fitted red hat emblazoned with a white *O*. While the crowd enjoyed him along with other antics, he did not come into iconic fame until 1924, when Sooners saw how much they needed him.

On a brisk October day, the football team, boosters and fans traveled to Des Moines, Iowa, to play against Drake University. The trip required changing trains in Arkansas City, Kansas. Somewhere in the commotion, Mex became separated from his compatriots. As the players took the field, the crowd began asking the same question that was plaguing Mott Keys: "Where's Mex?"

The game was a nightmare. Only a few years before, the Sooners had defeated Kingfisher College in a record-setting game, 179–0. Oklahoma football coach Bennie Owen, who had three undefeated seasons under his belt already in his career, had hit a rough patch in the early 1920s, but nothing like the Drake game. He had suffered three bigger shutouts before at the hands of Nebraska, Texas and Kansas, but a final score of 0–28 against a private school in Iowa was shocking. The fans and press agreed that fears for the missing Mex had caused the downfall.

A reward of fifty cents was offered for the return of Mex. Fans searched everywhere in Iowa, and several even left the game early to backtrack the journey. After several harrowing hours, J.D. Hull, Hughes B. Davis and J.C. Henley found Mex on the platform in Arkansas City, pacing back and forth and waiting. Jubilation flowed from Sooner fans and dog lovers around the nation. In games afterward, caretakers personally drove Mex to the game.

The football team's record turned around again, giving Bennie Owen two more winning seasons before he retired at the end of 1926. New coach Adrian Lindsey took the helm, and Mex continued to take up his place on the sidelines cheering on the team. After Lindsey's first season, on April 30, 1928, Mex died. He was fourteen years old, ninety-eight in dog years.

The whole city of Norman broke out in mourning. The campus closed, canceling all classes and events. Students, administration and city officials made plans for a public processional. On May 2, businesses in Norman closed, and thousands of people lined the streets as the small casket holding the body of Mex was marched to its final resting place on the sidelines of Owen Field.

The field has been redone numerous times along with construction on the Memorial Stadium, so it is unlikely that the body of Mex remains on the grounds. However, campus legend states that Mex is still among the crowds on game days. Players have claimed feeling their fingers being licked and quickly drawing them back to find no dog in sight. Coaching staff and press alike have felt something bump against their legs or even rest leaning against them like a well-behaved dog would. While some say that they can still hear Mex's barks when touchdowns are made, the roar of the stadium and the Roughneck rifles make it difficult to pick out a disembodied woof.

Whether the little canine ghost still roams the Sooner field or not, all fans feel certain that his spirit lives on in every game.

SELECTED BIBLIOGRAPHY

Books

Levy, David W. *The University of Oklahoma: A History.* Vol. 1. Norman: University of Oklahoma Press, 2005.

Articles

Bledsoe, Bob. "Haunters Exorcised in Norman?" *The Oklahoman*, September 24, 1973.

Chamberlain, John. "OU Probe Should Clear the Air." *The Oklahoman*, November 19, 1971.

Clay, Nolan, and Ty McMahan. "'I Truly Hang My Head....'" *The Oklahoman*, October 9, 2005.

Davis, Fred. "Coed Killed in 3-Story Fall from OU Fraternity House." *The Oklahoman*, February 7, 1972.

Eger, William. "Suicide Victim Had Sinister Plan." *The Oklahoman*, October 12, 2005.

Ellis, Randy, and Ty McMahan. "OU Blast Victim Raises Suspicions." *The Oklahoman*, October 6, 2005.

Fenwick, Ben. "DeBarr Faulted for Klan Ties." *The Oklahoman*, August 8, 1988.

Mathis, Nancy. "Sigma Chi Fire Victims Welcomed into Homes." *The Oklahoman*, August 19, 1980.

Mecoy, Don. "OU Police Say Elevator's Safety Devices Removed." *The Oklahoman*, August 11, 1986.

Medley, Robert. "Boardinghouse Owners 'Harassed.'" *The Oklahoman*, June 5, 1996.

———. "'Connections' Death Being Investigated." *The Oklahoman*, March 29, 1995.

———. "Ex-Patients Draw Complaints." *The Oklahoman*, June 3, 1996.

———. "Norman Man Charged in Decapitation Case." *The Oklahoman*, May 29, 1996.

Norman Transcript. "Main Building of the University Destroyed by Fire." December 26, 1907.

———. "No More Smallpox Here; Last Victims Ready for Release." December 15, 1922.

———. "Rumors We Have Heard." November 29, 1922.

———. "Students Confined in Infirmary Will Be Released Soon." December 5, 1922.

Oklahoma Daily. "Who You Gonna Call?" October 31, 2002.

The Oklahoman. "Fire Hits Second Frat House." December 19, 1983.

———. "OU Coed's Death Ruled an Accident." February 10, 1972.

OU Daily. "Duck Pond Reflects Changes." December 1, 1975.

Shelburne, Shorty, and Linda Maule. "200 Students View 12-Story Death Dive Off New OU Tower." *The Oklahoman*, September 23, 1967.

Sutter, Ellie. "Sorority Secrets Recalled." *The Oklahoman*, March 31, 2002.

Waddell, Karen. "Campus Police Call Dormitory Leap 'Suicide.'" *The Oklahoman*, April 5, 1971.

Websites

Alpha Chi Omega—Psi Chapter. "Alpha Chi Omega History." http://www.oualphachi.com/alpha-chi-omega-history.

Café Plaid. http://www.cafeplaid.com/Cafe_Plaid/Welcome.html.

Campus Corner. http://www.oucampuscorner.com/history.

College of Arts & Sciences, University of Oklahoma. "Haunted Ellison Hall: Paranormal Investigators Seek Roller Skating Boy." http://cas.ou.edu/haunted-ellison-hall-paranormal-investigators-seek-roller-skating-boy.

CRIS Contact Research Investigation Specialists. "Whitehand Hall, OU Campus." http://criscontactresearch.com/whitehand_hall.

Elmwood Funeral Home & Memorial Park. "Naydene B Daniel." http://www.elmwoodfuneral.com/services.asp?page=odetail&id=24919&locid=32.

News9. "OU Student Unaware She Was Pregnant Until She Gave Birth in the Dorm." http://www.news9.com/story/10545153/ou-student-unaware-she-was-pregnant-until-she-gave-birth-in-the-dorm.

Norman Masonic Lodge #38. "The Origins of Freemasonry in Norman, Oklahoma." http://www.normanlodge38.org/lodge_history.php.

Society of the Haunted. "Ellison Hall." http://www.societyofthehaunted.com/index.php/investigations/historic-haunts/103-ellison-hall.

SoonerSports.com. http://www.soonersports.com.

SoonerStats.com. http://www.soonerstats.com.

University of Oklahoma Police Notebook. "Friends of the Duck Pond." http://www.ou.edu/oupd/duckpond.htm.

About the Author

Jeff Provine is a farm kid turned college composition professor. After growing up on the family claim dating back to the Land Run of 1893, he attended the School of Science and Math before going on to complete his master's degree in professional writing at the University of Oklahoma. He writes webcomics, blogs regularly, campaigns for the integration of Internet media into the classroom and has developed courses on the history of comic books and the life of Charlie Chaplin. He has never seen a ghost. The standing rule for the ghost tour is that, if a ghost does appear, it is immediately canceled.

www.jeffprovine.com